How to bring up your parents

To our wives and children, who
have practised while we preached

© Nicholas & Camilla Gold Pty Ltd and
M.N.D.C. Publications Pty Ltd 1969

First published in Australia 1969 by Sun Books

First published in the United Kingdom 1980 by
THE MACMILLAN PRESS LTD
London and Basingstoke
Associated companies in Delhi Dublin
Hong Kong Johannesburg Lagos Melbourne
New York Singapore and Tokyo

Printed in Hong Kong

British Library Cataloguing in Publication Data

Gold, Stanley
  How to bring up your parents.
  1. Parent and child
  I. Title   II. Eisen, Peter
  301.42'7   HQ755.85

ISBN 0-333-29069-0

How to bring up your parents

Stanley Gold M.B., B.S., F.R.A.N.Z.C.P., D.P.M. (Lond.), M.R.C. Psych.

Peter Eisen M.B., B.S., F.R.A.N.Z.C.P., D.P.M.

M

This is where we begin

Now we are toddling

We are people

We go to school

We are no longer children

Foreword

Empathy is a beautiful word that fits a beautiful concept. It is, in many respects, a much better word than *sympathy*, especially in the latter's degenerate connotation of 'feeling sorry for'. Empathy is altogether less condescending and more sensitive. It involves a capacity for resonating with someone or something, of feeling *with*, and more exactly, of feeling *into*, as suggested by the German word *Einfuhlung*. Current theory sets the genesis of empathy in the early parent-child relationship. If the parents are empathetic with regard to the needs and feelings of their infant, he will undoubtedly grow up to become sensitive to the needs and feelings of others, and therefore become a better parent himself. In general, it is easier to develop empathy for someone like yourself with the same background and interests; difficulties arise, however, when this special sensitivity is required to bridge the gulf between sexes and generations. When it fails to do the job, a complex set of troubles may ensue characterised by much misunderstanding and much mis-management. The reason for this lies in the fact that developmentally empathy comes before understanding, and without that prior basis, there can be little growth of real understanding.

This book is an exercise in empathy in its most sensitive form. Two male adults, who take care of children and care for children, have attempted to feel into the inner life of small people from infancy to adolescence. Using empathy and technical knowledge, they have invaded the dark and nebulous caverns of the child's mind, speaking for the child in a way that sounds most authentic. The 'voice' they use is warm, comfortable, and colloquial, and by the time one has run through the various chapters, one has begun to develop quite a fond feeling for these wise and tolerant children who approach their parents with so much consideration and concern.

In attempting to speak for the child, the authors have shrewdly decided to project a 'voice' belonging to a single epoch, and they have understandably chosen adolescence as offering the most advantage. I will quote what they have to say about this themselves:

We've tried to broadly identify ourselves as intelligent adolescents; to write as if we were talking for children of all ages from the lofty perch of adolescence. From here we assume we can be close enough to childhood to comprehend its mysteries insightfully, involved in adolescence itself, and independent enough to be critical of adults. If we can assist some parents and some children to communicate with each other, we feel we will have contributed something of value.

It is this 'double orientation' of the adolescent, looking backward and at the same time forward, that gives the book a perspective that is just right. To have identified oneself with a younger child might have led to a different thing from the actual problems of parents encountered during child rearing. On the other hand, to have identified with the struggles of the father or mother might have put the child's point of view at a disadvantage. So many of the books written by parents, for parents, and to parents end by becoming didactic and admonitory, exploiting the ready sources of shame and guilt existent in all parents. What is unusual about this book is that there is very little reproachfulness in it. For this reason, and also for the fact that it is so largely based on empathy, I would prefer to recommend this book rather than Spock's to the new parents. It might make an excellent companion piece to Spock, since child care is approached from a different angle that should supplement the straight advice given by Spock. As befits the child's point of view, these authors have altogether a lighter touch, and therefore the often hidden advice may prove more palatable and acceptable. In this context, it is surprising how much dynamic theory the authors manage to pack into their book. It is clearly easier to take in theory from the mouths of babes and sucklings than from experts and certainly less threatening. The theory flows in smoothly in a functional way as the child discusses the probable sources of his disturbed behaviour. Surprising, too, is the amount of ground covered, ranging through almost every syndrome in child psychiatry. It is really a textbook in disguise, and for this reason might well exercise an even wider appeal to the medical students, teachers, child care workers, and others.

The whole tone of the book is such that many problems that parents may even find too distressing and revolting to discuss with their pediatrician are here introduced shorn of much of their fearfulness. The 'child' requests that his parents speak directly and unequivocally to him about 'secret' subjects, and he sets an example by speaking thus to them. However, even when he is at his most critical, he softens the impact of what he is saying by 'feeling' the reaction of the parent. For example, he says to them: 'In a way, I suppose it must be frightening to some of our parents to see us as a sort of mirror.' There is no doubt that the mirror of childhood reflects the attitude and behaviour of the parents very accurately. Sometimes, it may seem to some of the readers that our sensitive authors have over-empathised with the child. This may be especially so when they deal with the depressed child in his unloved, unwanted, lonely and empty state, particularly when they speak of the child who is 'nothing' because he gets 'nothing', but I feel that this is justified since it is the depression of children that is so often overlooked and misunderstood. It is important to sense the poignancy of the moment of emptiness when there seems nothing that the child can do about it. 'You go to Mother, and she is empty.' Even here, the authors introduce a ray of helpful sunshine that softens the implicit condemnation. The child, the eternal optimist, turns to his parent and says, 'But cheer up, we're children; we are growing, we are changing, and we are alive!' What a touching piece of reassurance for all parents at all times.

E. James Anthony, M.D.
Ittleson Professor of Child Psychiatry
Washington University School of Medicine

Preface

This book is not about disturbed children but rather about disturbances in children and in their relationships with their parents. Parents have always been interested in their children and in their behaviour. They have, however, often been puzzled and a little alarmed by some of the more impulsive actions of those who they after all see as smaller versions of themselves. Their reaction to this traditionally has been to restrict the activities of the 'little monsters' and to bring them up along rather strict, rigid and authoritarian lines.

Over recent years parents have been at first dismayed and then shocked to learn that some of the time-honoured child-rearing practices are inappropriate if not dangerous. All manner of difficulty in later life has been ascribed to developmental incidents and accidents in child-hood, and parents have as a consequence become mystified and apprehensive.

In their alarm and ignorance they have rushed for solace and information to a number of 'experts' who, sympathising and identifying with the beleaguered adults, have provided ample detail of an adults' eye view of children and their difficulties. Public opinion has at times run full circle, so that children, undisciplined and undirected, have wandered aimlessly and anxiously through some of the most important periods of their life; and, ultimately have often aggressively entered adolescence. At times the reaction has been retrogressive and cries of 'bring back the birch' have echoed through the land.

In all of this growing furore very few people have acknowledged the needs, wishes, thoughts, feelings and ideas of the children themselves. Their parents have successfully repressed and obliviated all memory of their own childhood and have refused to listen to what their own children have to say. One of the authors recently asked to speak in a discussion group entitled 'Your children, their problems and you' retitled his own contribution, 'You, your problems and your children', and it was from this beginning and discussions which subsequently followed that the present book took shape.

It is to be hoped that the thoughts expressed will be accepted in the manner in which they were intended, that of bringing parent and child closer together in their understanding and knowledge of each other.

We would like to express our grateful appreciation to all those who have been our colleagues and teachers over the years. Particularly, we would like to mention the Consultant Adult and Child Psychiatric Staff at Guy's Hospital, London, and Dr. W. S. Rickards, Director of the Department of Psychiatry, Royal Children's Hospital, Melbourne, whose enthusiasm and understanding have been an inspiration to us both.

Our sincere thanks are also due to Mrs. Margaret Gold for secretarial assistance in the preparation of the original manuscript.

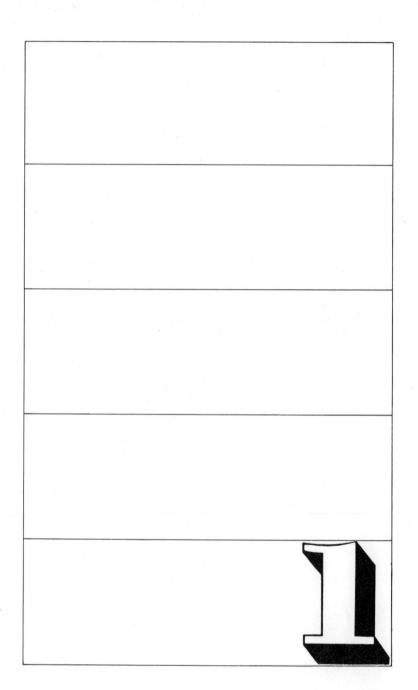

This is where we begin

How to help mother breast feed

One of the first things you meet after you get born might well be mother's breast. Sometimes (more in the olden days) it could be someone else's breast. That's what's called 'wet nursing', though I can't understand how it gets called that. Anyway, some of us get latched onto a nipple of a breast within minutes of our birth, others have to wait a few hours or even a few days. There are probably more changes in breast feeding habits than there are in fashions that mothers dress in. But despite all that, your first contact with the breast is likely to be a major event in your life. How you manage to start to suck, how you start to get milk and swallow it, and how you work out when you have had enough or want more, are kind of small mysteries that are just being worked out. There seems to be a sort of magic connected with breast feeding because for many of you, as well as a large number of mothers, breast feeding seems to be a way of solving all the ills of small mankind.

The first thing to decide is whether it is better to be breast fed or bottle fed. From mother's point of view there will be many kinds of reasons for her deciding for one or the other. From your point of view it's pretty hard to decide which you would prefer. It's your bad luck that at the time the decision is made about this important matter, you have no say in it. If you could have a say you would probably go for the thing that comes naturally to you. It seems that most (and probably all of us) have got a type of inbuilt homing device, zeroed in onto mother's breast and nipple. If we are given the general direction and are within range then we will probably 'home in'. This seems to be a natural way of doing things; probably it's helped by the presence of mum (in very close contact with us), the shape and feel of her breast, smell of her and possibly of her milk, and perhaps after a few days the shape and features of her face looking down on us. If you contrast this with the feel and shape of the bottle and teat, difference in make up (perhaps smell and taste) of cow's, goat's or other kinds of milk, and the difference in the way of holding you for you to get onto the bottle, then it's likely that bottle feeding might not 'feel' as natural and perhaps as comfortable to you. Unfortunately for you it's probably not as simple as this; the way that mothers feel and the way in which these feelings are passed on to you probably determines how you will get on with the breast.

Many of your mothers will want to breast feed you. However, nowadays it seems, this kind of feeding is not used as often as it could be.

The way in which mother feels about breast feeding controls the way in which she goes about it. You will probably get on best if mother holds you quite firmly in the position from which you can grab hold of the nipple, brush her breast with your hand, kick your feet and watch her face all at the same time. You'll feel good if she manages to give all her attention to you, not to have to worry about doing anything else at feeding time, not be in a hurry to finish and be able to herself enjoy your feeding. As against this, some mothers find breast feeding not so pleasant, try to read a book, have a sleep, look after your older brother or sister, or even knit whilst they are holding and feeding you. If mother can't concentrate on this feeding you are likely to be aware of her tension or even of her being rather unwilling to breast feed you. For some of you this will be the beginning of a time of doubt, of being unsure of whether mother is really with you or not. Because we rely on her so much in having our feelings of hunger satisfied and of being held, nursed, and feeling secure, when this doesn't happen we have every right to get annoyed and upset. Sometimes to show we are annoyed we squirm during our feed or don't latch on quickly, and stay on the nipple, or perhaps we cry, pushing at mum's breast and refusing to feed, or later on by biting instead of sucking. If these or other things happen you might not only show mum that you are annoyed, but also annoy her. Then she gets more tense, less patient and you're in even worse trouble than before. Probably, even when you are only a few weeks or months old, you are capable of working out what's right for you in the way of feeding and what's not right. Mostly mothers get onto the right way very quickly, then everything goes well. But should they and you not click then troubles seem to pile one on top of the other.

What's likely to happen is that mother will get down in the dumps about her role as a breast feeder. She might think that it's all her fault and that she is not much good. At times mothers are quite glad when trouble over breast feeding starts, because they really don't want to feed. They might say to themselves, 'My milk is not really strong enough,' or 'He is not getting enough milk from me,' or even 'My milk is not good enough milk, it's bad for baby,' and stop breast feeding. This helps some mothers because it's what they really want. Others feel sad and guilty and don't function too well for a time because they've stopped doing something for you that they reckon they should be doing.

Usually we handle the process of weaning quite well if it's reasonably planned and carried out. However, if mother should decide overnight that she is going to stop, or if her milk runs out suddenly (because she has had a shock or been ill or lost interest), then we often wonder very much about what's going on. We lose the best pacifier we've had, lose the time of close contact with mum and often fear that we've not only lost mum's breast feeding, but also that we've lost her. Screaming day and night, refusing to drink from the bottle or cup, or vomiting, even if you don't drink, are ways you might use to tell mum that you're not happy about your loss. Usually you will get used to the idea after a few days or weeks. Some of you find this harder and might feel so hurt that you reckon that the world is a bad place to live in and withdraw a bit from it. Probably all of you who have had to be weaned suddenly will remember it in one way or another, just as you probably remember being breast fed as a major event in your lives so far.

It's probably fair to most mothers who breast feed their baby to say that they will decide the right time to stop and decide it quite well. Sometimes, however, we may decide this for them; by refusing to keep on sucking from mother. Perhaps we have got to the stage of wanting to be a bit independent, usually at around eight or nine months or so, or we have found out about other kinds of food, like meat, vegetables, etc. If you can stop at the time mum wants you to, it's probably because you and she are already in pretty good harmony.

It's this business of mother's feelings and the way that your feelings reflect hers that is one of the biggest aspects of breast feeding. It is true to say that you will never get closer to your mum than when she is breast feeding you (that is, other than the time you were inside her). If mother loves to breast feed then you will know this. On the other hand, if she does not like breast feeding and only does it because it's said to be good for you you'll also know it, and probably not feel as good.

There are really two things that are essential for us to benefit from breast feeding. A contented and happy mother and a contented and happy baby. Mother really needs to want to breast feed and needs to get pleasure and satisfaction and the feeling of warmth and goodness from it. If she does do that, she is pretty sure to handle us right and hold us right, to know more or less without even thinking about it that she is giving us more than just food. She will be able to give it the right way and at the right times without any troubles. That is of course so long as we are contented as she is. If we are angry or greedy or crying, or if we have different sorts of physical things wrong that stop us from sucking or swallowing things properly, then even the contented mother pretty soon loses her patience and it's no wonder. I am sure lots of our mothers would be reassured to know that we understand the way that they feel, and that we would not expect them to breast feed us if they really feel unhappy about it, for one reason or another. The most important thing for us really is that they should feel happy and secure in what they do, especially to us. Because if they are happy and contented then so will we be. But mother needs to be happy and willing to breast feed, to be well enough and strong enough, to be reasonably sure to be able to give time and interest to breast feeding us, and to be able to get help, both for herself and us, should something go wrong.

If we could talk to our mothers they would be greatly encouraged by what we would say, and often they need some of this encouragement, and sometimes some guidance, and shouldn't be afraid to ask for it. After all mothers are not natural cows and it takes time to learn how.

How to handle your parents when you are vomiting

It's never fun to vomit. Mothers don't like children to do it, fathers think it's dirty. No-one, but no-one, ever sees it as funny. There does seem to be something serious about vomiting. I suppose when we think back it's pretty hard to remember ever vomiting and liking it. Most things seem to have a good side to them—but not vomiting. Vomiting is also called 'being sick' and this always has a bad sound to it. There are usually lots of ways of doing most things, except vomiting. In fact most people you know, if you ask them to talk about vomiting, will probably look at you with that special kind of look that means you are something different, queer or revolting. Seldom will you find mixed with that look sympathy or understanding. Now, that seems strange because you would reckon that anybody who could remember vomiting would be a bit sympathetic to anyone else who is vomiting, and everybody vomits. The answer might be that everybody feels something bad connected with vomiting. When we are babies, all of us vomit at some time or other. Of course it's called by lots of different names, like spitting, spilling, possetting and chucking, but it all means the same thing. Vomiting really only has one aim, to get rid of something. So no matter how we try to hide it behind different names, we can't get away from its real purpose. You won't ever have noticed a baby smile and vomit at the same time. When we do vomit we never have that calm, settled, peaceful look about us, although sometimes we don't seem to object much to playing with, touching, puddling in or even rolling in pools of vomit, although that's a different sort of thing. It seems that the act of vomiting is a bad thing. When we are very young we often have more simple feelings about vomiting than those that come to us when we get older, and certainly much more simple than parents'. When we are babies it's simply a matter of saying, 'That stuff in there is no good, if it's not good it's not doing me any good, and as I can't stand anything that makes me feel bad, the only thing to do is to get rid of it, so here goes, vomit.'

It would be very nice if vomiting stayed just like that, getting rid of something bad, but it doesn't. The trouble is there are lots of things that are bad and lots of situations that are bad and lots of times that are bad and even more, lots of feelings that are bad. Vomiting gets pretty important as a way of getting rid of all these different kinds of bad. The trouble is that vomiting finds it a bit hard to discriminate between different kinds of bad, so it acts the same way for all of them. If you are up to about three or four months old the least likely thing will be that you're 'sick', that is, sick in your body. You might have a blockage in your stomach or an infection somewhere or a twisted tube, or a blocked hole or something, but more than likely you'll be 'sick' in another way—sick of something, rather than sick with something. You might be sick of the way your milk supply is jet propelled or, worse still, how it does not come on time, or at the right rate and with the right feelings. This last thing, not getting milk with the right feelings, is very likely to make you sick because it will always make you feel bad if your food is given to you to shut you up, or to stop you crying, or to keep you quiet. It probably is most likely that you will be 'sick' because you feel that something is wrong with your world. If anything at all goes wrong it is likely that you feel bad, so to get rid of bad, vomit. In this baby world just about the most important person after yourself is mother. If she feels bad (translated for adults into depressed, anxious, bored, dejected, irate, furious and lots of other feelings) then as she is part of our world we feel bad along with her. Even if she gives us the right kind of milk at the right time, rate and flow, with the best of intentions, mixed with that milk will be a bit of bad, so up it comes.

Even most doctors don't seem to know about this business of baby's bad feeling making them vomit. They do, however, seem to have some kind of sixth sense that tells them it's got to do with 'nerves', so they try to help with nerve medicine, or, as they call it, a sedative. You'd think they'd know better and instead of giving it to us they might try giving it to our mothers. Sometimes if they look hard and wide enough they might even find it is not mother who needs it, it is father or grand-mother or even auntie. These other people might all feel bad and by their way of behaving they cause mother to feel bad, and so then we do.

It is really possible to get very confused over this business of how bad feelings spread around. For example, as a baby you would think you would almost be right in saying to yourself that you are the centre of your world. Being in the centre means that everything and everybody around you can look at you, touch you and more than anything else get at you. Being a baby you will probably stir up different kinds of feelings in all the various people you come in contact with. Some of them will love you, some will hate you, some might tolerate you and others ignore you. Some could be critical of you, a great number could praise you. Even more than that, your being a baby always changes the way of life of everyone around you. Most people don't like their lives being changed or if they have to have it changed they like to be able to do all the changing themselves. Anger, frustration, annoyance, envy and rage may all simmer in a big pot of feelings, with you in the centre of it. These feelings get to be part of your world and they are always uncomfortable to live with. As you want more than anything else to be comfortable and at peace, it is not hard to see being uncomfortable is a bad feeling, a feeling of people or things or something getting at you. To get rid of it you will probably try the best way you know to make bad feelings go away the quickest, that is, vomiting. It might sound to you as if every baby has bad feelings and that every baby vomits when it feels bad. Well, this is really only partly true. As you know some of us do it a whole lot, and others do it only very rarely. If we are always vomiting it often means that there is a lot of bad feeling going around in our relatives. But if we only do it now and then it's likely that our families are pretty nice and stable with just a few bits of worry and occasional bad feeling. No matter where we live or who looks after us, we pretty soon learn one basic rule—vomiting is no fun.

This rule stays with us all our lives. As we grow older we are more likely to vomit only if we are 'real' sick, but we can always go back to using vomiting as a way of getting rid of bad feelings like we learnt when we were babies. You will find that vomiting can be used as a threat, particularly if you don't want to go somewhere or do something.

If you say you are going to vomit or even make a few noises which sound pretty ominous, or perhaps if you really get carried away and put your finger at the back of your throat and start to vomit, you are certain to get some response from your parents. Knowing as we do that no-one likes vomiting, you can be almost as certain that your parents will do anything you want to stop you vomiting. It's just as well our bluff isn't called too often because we don't like all the mess any better than anybody else.

To be fair to parents, they are at a disadvantage every step of the way in this business of vomiting. When you are babies you might frequently vomit on mother's dress, the kitchen floor, the lounge-room carpet and occasionally on father's freshly dry-cleaned trousers. This kind of vomit is not too hard to clean up. By the time you get to solid foods the vomit changes to a much less agreeable kind. It smells. At this age you might vomit almost anywhere, but I can bet that someone else will have to get rid of the mess. Children of four and five seem to have the knack of vomiting in bed, usually at night and always a sufficient amount to make it necessary to change the sheets or blankets. I have even heard of older children and grown ups vomiting at someone else, which is about the most angry thing one can think of doing. But it is strange, where parents can hit, bite, pinch, swear at or even wee on their children if that is what their child does to them, they usually cannot bring themselves to vomit back even though they sometimes feel like doing it.

If there is one thing it would be nice to feel that our parents could learn from our vomiting, it would be that it comes from these bad things inside of us, whether it's bad food, bad milk or bad feelings. They can always make us feel better if they really want to, and we will always be grateful if they can offer us other ways of letting them know how we feel. But I have no doubt that both our parents and ourselves heave a great sigh of relief when we get old enough to be able to talk properly, and express ourselves properly, so that when we get 'fed up' we can just go to them and say, 'You make me sick.'

How to manage your parents if you are having feeding difficulties

No matter if you got it from your mother's breast or from a bottle your main diet for the first few months will have been milk. It should be a pretty simple process for you to get your milk, get enough of it, get it at the right time, in the right place and by the right way of eating. However, these simple things seem to get pretty confused at times.[1]

What we reckon about how milk tastes, especially if we like it or not, never seems very important. Milk is what we are supposed to have, so milk is what we get for quite a time; in fact some of us will probably drink milk for a very, very long time, because there seems to be some kind of idea that by drinking milk you stay healthy. There are so many people who later in their lives hate milk and even so many kids who won't drink it, that maybe it is not as good as it is made out to be, or maybe it is because as babies we are pretty much made to drink milk so that later on we revolt a bit and say 'no' to drinking it.

This being made to drink milk is a bit like a law. In fact there seem to be quite a few laws about what to eat and how much to eat, particularly for babies. There are a whole lot of women whom babies can never understand. These women get the baby every week or so, undress them, put them on a cold dish and wiggle the dish around until the baby feels that he will fall off and so startles and begins to cry. Then these women go into a lot of talk about formulas and ounces and not enough milk, not quite enough flow, too big a hole and so on till not only babies are crying, but so is mum. This performance keeps going on even though babies and mothers don't really like it. It's just part of the rules of the game. Some other rules seem to apply to whether you can be over-fed or under-fed. It is somehow taken for granted that just like a bucket can continue to overflow if too full or carry more if half empty so should we. Somehow I doubt if any baby could be over-fed like a bucket. Eventually you would either shut your mouth or stop sucking or bring it all up like a fountain. On the other hand you could get under-fed, especially if mum sticks to the rules, such as if you're so big and so old you should only drink that number of ounces. If you seem to want more it's supposed to be only because you're greedy. Maybe it's nothing to do with hunger, it's just the wind or the colic that makes you scream, or at least so they say. In fact you will probably get pretty disturbed if your mother and even perhaps your father, but almost certainly your grandmother(s) insist that you only eat according to the rules. We don't really know much about rules at this age, only the ones that say, 'I feel good when I'm full and not good when I'm

[1] See *How to help mother breast feed.*

empty,' 'The best way to make me feel good is to let me have mum to suck on till I fall asleep.' Somehow these things that you believe in seem to get replaced with sayings like 'you've got to put on X ounces in Y days', 'you must double your birth weight by the time you're so old', 'a weigh a day keeps the doctor away'.

Rules get even more hard to follow when it comes to deciding when we should eat. Here there are changing fashions we have to contend with. There are two big words, 'demand' and 'by-the-clock', neither of which we are expected to understand, which is just as well since I don't think many parents do either. To us hunger is just a feeling and an unpleasant feeling that comes and gets more unpleasant, and more and even more unpleasant as time goes on. It isn't really that we can stick to a clock, nor that we can demand our food. What we can do is show how unpleasant we feel because this hungry thing makes us feel all tensed up. Now food makes you feel more content, but it's got to be food delivered by the right person, in the right way, with the right kind of feeling and techniques, not just food on time or when you 'demand' it. It's not just so simple as demand or not demand. It's all the things that go with it that count. If they have to have a system, why couldn't it be the 'making baby feel good' system?

A part of most systems of feeding seems to be concerned with where you should eat. It is pretty easy while we are small because there is really only one way in which you can eat and that's being held in someone's arms. Even if this is the only way, some people are prepared to argue with this rule and try to feed us while we are lying down, in our cot, straddled over a pillow or even 'sitting up in a chair'. One of these ways of breaking the rule is to 'prop' the bottle. This is a pretty good device for someone who has lots of work to do and can't spend much time in feeding. It's kind of considered as neither here nor there that we don't really know how much work goes on around us, neither do we care about it, but we do care if we are not held while we feed.

Once you can sit up you are placed in a chair especially made for you, because you are really the centre of attention. This special chair is where you eat and are also at times supposed to empty your bowels and bladder. Again it's a bit like not being held when you are a baby, because after all every time you look down you nearly have a fit of fear that you'll fall. Sometimes you do. Still most of you make out in time and use your special chair for all sorts of tricks. It's a particularly good place from which to throw food, drop plates, spill drinks and hurl spoons.

Just when is the time for you to graduate from your special chair to a chair at the table will depend on a few things—like how much your parents are prepared to put up with your way of eating, how they feel about your growing up (being at the table with them is really being the same as them). It is pretty certain that for us getting to a grown up's table will be a big thrill—something we look forward to for a long time and something we will probably regret for many days ahead.

This is because our precarious high seat kind of gave us licence to eat anyway we wanted to. But once you get to be grown up you've got to eat according to the rules. Fingers are made for picking food up, mouths, teeth, tongue for chewing, slurping, licking, and other un-nameable activities. If you should dare bring with you these rather natural activities, you'll probably be quickly reminded of your animal forebears, and your parents in the heat of the moment forget that they themselves are your forebears, and threaten you with expulsion to eating with pigs, dogs or at the zoo (this prospect of course we often relish). Instead of allowing you to eat naturally, your parents, who are aided and abetted by eating utensils manufacturers, will present you with an array of increasingly more complex and inappropriate devices. These are so designed that with our greasy fingers we can't really get a grip of them. They have such small surfaces that our rudimentary sense of balance tends to cause all the food to slip off before we can get it into our mouth. The drinking arrangements are equally hard to manage: tiny openings where lumps cannot come out of or get stuck in, unspill-able lead-bottom cups that are so heavy we can't lift them and so on. It's no wonder that we get frustrated over this business of grown-up eating and revert to natural eating. It's even more of a wonder that eventually we come to accept grown-up eating habits. Probably this is only because we want to pay a compliment to our parents on their excellent table manners. Luckily this is what most of us will do. It's pretty hard for parents to understand that this may take the best part of ten or twelve years. I kind of suspect that they really only find it hard because this means they have to watch their table manners so as to set us a good example and they probably get a bit sick of doing this and wish they could eat naturally too.

When you've come to the time of being allowed to eat in places like restaurants you'll probably hear your parents tell their friends what a joy it is to take you out, how nice it is that you never disgrace them by eating with your fingers. But there are still a number of ways with which you can show mother and father that you are not really perfect feeders as yet. One way is to refuse to eat. You could start this real early on, especially if you had troubles over eating as a baby, or perhaps if you're angry with them for any of a lot of reasons. You'll find that not eating will get your parents to feel quite unhappy. Some parents get pretty anxious if you will not eat, they think you will starve or that you won't grow. Other mothers and fathers might feel what's called guilty because through your not eating you're not going along with their way of giving you something important. Just as you learn that food is something that mum gives you and so you kind of accept food as coming from mum, or being part of her, so does mum feel that she is providing you with the goods or, in other words, with love, by giving you nice things to eat. You might not like her all the time, or worse still not know how you can both like her and be angry with her. This is a kind of confusing idea to get hold of and used to. If it is particularly hard you could refuse to eat for her as a way of showing her you don't trust your feelings (perhaps because you can't trust her feelings for you). Sometimes not eating gets so bad we go on strike altogether. Hunger strikes are ways that even adults have of getting something done or of showing the world just how strongly they feel about something that's important to them. They know just as we do that eating is a very important way of making friends but also of showing who are your enemies. Since adults won't eat with their enemies, why should we?

Sometimes it is not a real strike, just a bit of one centred around certain kinds of food. This way of selecting some food not to eat is called Food Fads. If you look around you will see that everyone has got these. Some people like marrow, pumpkin, horse radish, lambs' fry, sheep's brains and other similar kinds of food. Yet other people can't stand eating them. There are usually hidden reasons for a particular food not being eaten. You'll notice that many fads are over foods that come from particular parts of animals or grow in rather different ways from the common types of food we eat. You know it's very strange that most parents complain about their children having food fads, yet are quite unaware that they themselves won't eat certain kinds of food. Often, an identical pattern of likes and dislikes that they see as a fad with us is just one of those things for themselves.

There are kinds of not eating that are called fads without really being so. All of us will eat ice cream, cake, biscuits, sweets, lemonade, and so on rather than wait for meal times and then eat meat and vegetables.

When I say *all* of us that is except some children, like children of
Dentists who are not allowed to be like other children and eat sweet
things, even though they would really love to do so. If you are an
unhappy or depressed child you will probably eat very large quantities
of sweets and not eat anything else. It might even be that your parents
kind of encourage you to eat sweets by sending you to the corner shop
to buy a packet of cigarettes and yourself a reward. Sometimes you are
given pocket money and if you can get away with it you may spend it
all on sweets. Then along comes dinner and to your parents' surprise
you can't eat your meal. It's not fair to you and you are not fair to your
parents. You should really grow up more quickly so that you learn to
deny yourselves pleasure, or at least put it off until a more appropriate
time to have it. If we could do this perhaps we would have less
arguments at meal times.

If you work it out, a very large part of our lives is spent eating and
getting ready to eat. It is almost like a law that three meals a day is what
we must have. Because eating is such an important part of our lives, it
sometimes becomes over important and sometimes has tied up with it
lots of different meanings. What our parents don't perhaps realise is
that we don't really get upset if they set reasonable limits for us with
our eating, and other things for that matter. So long as they persist in
presenting us with a wide variety of foods and are firm, but not over
fussed or over anxious about it, things will probably work themselves
out pretty well.

After all, for most of us food and eating can be lots of fun. The main
trouble arises when food, feeding and meal times become so important
that they end up the centre of a battlefield on which we and our parents
are fighting. When this happens all the time, it's enough to make you
lose your appetite.

How to teach your parents what it means if you cry too much

When you first hear it, crying sounds all the same, but once you get
used to it, you learn that crying can mean lots of different things. No
matter what it means, crying always has the same effect on people. It
makes them take notice.

Crying is the first thing we learn to do. There used to be the idea that
all babies had to be spanked as soon as they got born, because that made

them breathe properly. So crying somehow gets all tied up with just being alive. It always has the effect of getting us noticed so we could say it's really a signal. This is where the experts reckon they can tell the difference between lots of kinds of signals. (Experts are mothers and also other grown ups who reckon they are just as good as mothers and so end up being baby-care Sisters, Kindergarten Supervisors, Children's Doctors and Child Psychiatrists.) These signals do seem a bit hard to get to know about, probably harder than learning about morse code and flag waving and things like that. Maybe it's just that it's hard to remember being a baby and so it's hard to understand really properly. In fact, I reckon that even children get a bit confused over what cry means which signal.

Babies all get hungry. Usually they cry as soon as they get hungry and they keep on crying until they are not hungry any more. But some babies get so hungry that even when they have finished feeding (in between bouts of crying), they still cry. By now it's probably not that they are hungry but frustrated, or angry, or something like that. Mostly crying for hunger starts as a signal that it's time for eating. This can get to be almost as good as a clock in telling the time, but if mother gets the idea (usually from other experts) that feeding ought to be by the clock and not according to when the baby is hungry, it might even work out that we never learn how to signal our hunger. That does not matter much until we get into the hands of an all-powerful waiter in a restaurant who does not somehow recognise our rather polite but inept signals for his attention.

When we are babies we also cry to get attention. By crying we learn that mother will come to us. Maybe it does not start as a cry for attention, but as a signal of hunger, so we get the idea that you can get both through the same kind of noise. Once we get real experienced at crying we can kind of control just when we want to be with someone and when we want to be alone. Being alone is all right for small amounts of time, but most of us can't stand it for too long. It's a funny thing, but many of our parents reckon we are happy to be alone, that we really enjoy lying under the trees in our pram or on the lounge-room floor with no-one else there. They even say how good we are if we can do this thing for long, long hours. What they don't really know is that we don't like to be lonely. They are only using it as an excuse so that they don't have to spend so much time with us. It's up to us to use our attention-getting signals only at the right times, but after all this takes a fair bit of practice. Until we are good at it, we expect attention most of the time or at least at those times when the experts say we are allowed to have it.

Not getting attention, just like not getting food, can be a pretty frustrating business. After a while we learn that being frustrated is another thing to cry about. It kind of lets people know that they are expected to do something for us. It's probably this kind of cry which is the hardest to do anything about. As soon as we let it out we may get a bottle stuck in our mouths or get picked up and rocked or have a bangle jangled so close it feels as if it is going to poke out an eye. It's somehow never the right things that are done, because there isn't really anything that anyone can do about us being frustrated. This is the worst thing for adults—they get to running about in circles, or standing on their heads out of their own frustrated desire to do something. They feel they have to do something because if they don't they might feel bad or guilty or they may reckon they are failures as parents or they may just be unable to stand the noise. It's a signal all right this crying because of frustration, but it means steer clear, let us work it out for ourselves.

Pain makes us cry and we every time invariably always mean it as an urgent signal. It can't sound like anything else, but it gets to be mistaken for other things. Lots of things cause pain. The pain might come from anywhere. We don't really know for sure how to tell which part of us is an arm or a bottom or our back or our bowel or our throat, especially when we are very young. It does not matter where the pain starts, it always feels the same because it gets to spread right through the whole of us and that can be a very bad feeling to have. It's only after quite a while that we can sort of learn how to fix up pain ourselves. After we have cried out and our parents come, time goes by and we feel a bit better. So later we get the idea each time we get a pain not to cry or just to cry a bit. Then we kind of pretend our parents are there and wait. Some of us never learn that our cry of pain is only a signal and kind of use the crying itself as a way of forgetting about the pain. This is usually by turning the crying into another kind, an angry cry.

When we are babies we all get angry, but adults often don't believe it. They look at us lying flat on our backs, kicking, screaming, going red in the face, screwing up our faces and eyes and say, 'isn't he sweet?' How out of touch can you get? It's probably because most people find it hard to handle angry feelings that they pretend that when we are babies we are much too sweet and good (in adults' talk they would say innocent) to feel anger. But we do, and how! Anger is one of the most common things to tell about through crying. We can really make our presence felt when we cry with anger. Because we might not just cry, but scream. If people don't get the message it makes us even more angry and we might be able to go on and on, even for hours. It's funny, but even if they don't seem to get the message that we are angry, our angry crying makes our parents very angry themselves. Without knowing why they might pick us up and squeeze us tight or shake us or throw us down into our cot or some equally unpleasant thing and then our crying turns into a cry of fear.

It is most likely that fear will come because of what adults do to us. So much are we tied up with and close to our parents that anything they do to jolt us out of our pleasant easy way of life can make us cry with fear. But this fear can also come from other things in our world. Things like loud noises, bright lights, cold wind, fast movements . . . all of those really make us cry because we don't know enough of what is going on and reckon it could be dangerous. Mostly it is not that these kind of things are really dangerous, but we don't know that. This being not sure is much harder for us children to put up with than it is for our parents. They have got used to telling the difference between what is really dangerous and what isn't and so they don't cry out with fear so much. But it's also strange how our cry, because of fear, makes our mother and father behave in an odd sort of way, as if they are frightened too. It's this getting to know how other people feel, and starting to get used to the way we feel ourselves, that often makes us cry and some-times makes us cry too much.

Right from early on, maybe even when we are only a few days or weeks old, we get to know what the place we live in is like. A big part of this baby world is made up of feelings. We learn to get used to our own feelings of a nice kind, like feelings of love, warmth and peace and we also get to learn of our angry, hostile and unsettling feelings. Much of this learning comes from our copying feelings we find other people have. Mother particularly is important here. She feels good and bad, loving hating, peaceful and angry, and we get to know just exactly how she feels, because we are so closely tied to her, especially in our early days and weeks and months. So if we find that our feelings get uncomfortable for us, kind of too many feelings or too strong feelings, we cry. Maybe we get angry, very often because we keep on being frustrated or we keep on being hungry or we don't get enough attention, and then these things happen more often than the nicer side of being full and in pleasant company and only sufficiently frustrated to keep life interesting. If that is so, it is very likely that we will cry, cry and cry. After a while we reckon that the world we live in is not a very nice place and even that it is a place that does not seem to like us. We might even begin to feel that the world is against us and that everybody else hates us or is very angry with us. That's enough to make anyone cry a lot, especially a little baby.

There are other sorts of feelings we get as babies, feelings that sometimes our parents are sure they don't communicate to us and we wish they didn't. Feelings like them being panicky and not knowing what to do with us; or feelings that sometimes they even hate us. Sometimes they will show us that they feel this way, but at other times they even seem to be very special kinds of parents, always looking after us and always doing good things for us and never openly getting angry with us. But all the same we can feel the angry ideas and feelings and this makes us sad and we cry. Or sometimes even worse, when they don't take any notice no matter how much we cry, we stop crying but also stop learning how to love anybody and really believe that it is not only mother who is against us, but the whole world.

Of course a lot of us cry when we are getting to be close to a year old if we are left by our mothers, sometimes even when she just disappears from our sight and goes out of the room and we can't feel she is with us any more. Now we have to learn that we are separate and it's a frightening feeling and so we scream. Although this happens to all of us, only some of us cry too much because of it. This is usually when our mothers themselves are somehow pretty worried about being separated from us.

It is not only mothers we have to be interested in if we want to learn to be separate, but also other kinds of people. Some people we kind of get used to easily, for instance, fathers (but only fathers who live with us instead of living at the office or business). It's also usually easy to get used to others like sisters, brothers, grandparents and relatives and maybe even the lady next door and the nappy wash man, but not strangers. Now most of us find it pretty hard to look at strangers without crying, especially when we are around seven to ten months or so old. You would think that strangers have something wrong with them and to us they have. They don't fit into our world that we slowly got used to and they look dangerous because they don't. So we are afraid of them and show it by crying too much. Luckily for our parents' social lives, as well as for the business of their day-to-day living, we get used to strangers after a while and then mothers can again go shopping, play bridge, or entertain their old girlfriends.

It's a very hard business for our parents to learn what our crying might mean. But somehow or other they have just got to try and learn our signals and know what it is that we want, or anyway what it is that we need. We don't really intend them to be frightened or upset or bluffed by us, although they are often all three. Whatever the reason for our crying may be, the one thing that it always means is that we need our parents some way or another, and this is something that we would like to feel that they understand, even if everything else is a bit confused.

Of course as we grow up the same kind of reasons for crying are still there, but we get to be able to talk back and behave so as to let other people know what we think and feel, so we don't need to cry so much. Crying is something we always seem to be getting into trouble about. We feel, particularly when we are young, that we need to cry often, and our parents say we don't. They don't really like us to cry and, to be honest, one of the reasons that we get to like it is because we find it is a way of getting what we want. Even when we grow up a bit, we still might use crying to say we are angry or frustrated or afraid or even lonely, but more often than not we are really saying, 'I want, give it to me and if you don't I will cry until it drives you mad'.

It really takes an expert like some mothers to be able to tell what our cry is all about. Mothers usually get to be expert, not only because they see us crying a lot, but because they use this business of crying to get what they want. If you don't believe me just ask your dad.

How to stop your parents worrying over your wind and poos

Almost everything that happens to us in our first few months seems to be tied up with wind. At least that is the impression that some grown ups have. They blame almost every kind of our behaviour from smiling to crying, not sleeping to snoring, spitting, hunger, head rolling, sweating and lots of other things on wind or colic. This colic must be a pretty potent thing if it can really cause all this. Somehow I don't believe it. Still, so many people, particularly parents, reckon it can do a lot of damage (usually to their own peace of mind). This business of wind is tied up pretty closely to feeding and vomiting and crying.

The first thing to decide is what wind really is and how it starts. Nobody really seems to know. Colic is pain, if you reckon that babies feel it the same way as grown ups do. Colic is a thing that makes us squirm and pull our legs up and then bend over double. It certainly seems to start in our insides and to be something to do with our stomach and bowel, but that's all it is. It is not something magic or very mysterious or supernatural. Colic does not start because of the temperature of milk or the size of our mouth or the shape of the teat or even the amount of milk we drink. It does start because of the air that gets caught up in our insides, but just how much air is needed and how it gets there is hard to say. Since we can't be sure what it is I suppose we can't be too hard on people who think all kinds of queer ideas about what's going on inside us when we have wind.

Still if parents and other grown ups see us with colic they sometimes say things like, 'It's the devil inside him,' 'Poor little fellow, he is bedevilled by wind,' 'It's all the colliwobbles getting stirred up,' and so on. When they say this they pretend to say it like a joke to make us feel better, but they are really only trying to make themselves feel better. They reckon that by making a joke of it they might have less fear of their own. Just in the same way all kinds of magic ways of fixing colic or wind get thought up. We don't really care what our parents do to us as long as they get rid of the colic, but we do care if in trying to get rid of the colic they give us something else that hurts or makes us feel sick. Some kinds of gripe water are almost like witch's brew and serve the same purpose. Banging on the back for long hours at a time gives us no chance to sleep it off, to get rid of the wind by being quiet and relaxed. Throwing us around really is a way of making us get more wind and that is even worse. Flannel around our middle, even if it is a beautiful red colour, does not do much except make us sweat. So we would like our parents not to do any of these kinds of things.

It would be best if they did not get too excited about us having colic and especially if they did not start thinking of colic every time we do something a bit different than sleep and eat. Mostly we feel colic in the night-time. It might just be that it is more at that time, not because of our fast greedy eating some eight or ten hours ago, but because mother is usually tired by that time of day. In fact just the way she feels might have more to do with our getting colic than anything else. Colic is one of those things that grown ups like to talk about. They get all kinds of stories called 'old wives' tales', passed down to one lot of them from another. If our mother is pretty unsure of herself she will already be a bit frightened, she will hold us differently and feed us very, very carefully and make sure we don't gulp our food and things like that. It's just that kind of care that should make us swallow a lot of air and then give us wind. But of even more importance to us is the way that mother thinks about pain—what it feels like to her and how good she is at putting up with it. Some mothers, just like some children, have funny ideas of what makes pain. Because we are pretty important to mother, when we get colic and pain she might kind of feel that our having pain is just the same as if she had it herself. Then she treats our pain just like she does her own. She might panic because to her pain is like a knife sticking into her inside or something like that, and when she panics so do we, and so our colic gets worse.

Sometimes colic gets so bad it seems to do something to our poos. It might seem that if we have a lot of colic we also should make a lot of poos. No-one will tell us, ever, just how much poos we are supposed to do and how often. Even if they won't tell us I wish they would tell our parents. There are two kind of things that go wrong with our poos that get our parents pretty excited. Either we make too much and too soft or watery poos, or we don't make enough and at the right time, often enough and soft enough. It is not very often that you hear your mother say, 'That's nice poos you have done,' or 'Doesn't he do poos nicely'. So maybe we should assume that most of us fit in to these two kinds of pooers—too much or not enough. That would almost be a pretty good way of dividing up all kinds of people, into good and bad pooers. Anyway, if we don't do enough poos or if it is pretty hard when it comes out, then we are what is called constipated.

To get constipated seems to be what happens to most of us at some time or other. Our parents have lots of different ideas about what constipation means. To us it's pretty simple—we just hold on to our poos. There might be a few reasons to do that but basically it's got the same result. Early on, when we are very little babies, poos just come and go almost without us knowing about it. It is after a few weeks or months that we notice a feeling in our bottoms, like some thing moving inside us.

We get used to the idea that if we push and grunt the feeling will go away and at the same time another feeling comes in a hole in our bottoms. That can be a nice feeling or a bad feeling. It gets to be a bad feeling if the lining of our bottoms has got split by a hard bit of poos. That hurts. Sometimes it hurts so much we kind of tighten up our bottoms, so much we stop the poos from coming out. Then we wake up to the idea that if we don't let our poos out it does not hurt, and that sometimes makes us constipated.

A bit later in our lives we might also learn how to hold on to our poos. This happens expecially when we find that our parents are anxious over this business of doing poos. If they keep at us to do poos or tell us to push it out or keep us sitting on the pot, we just don't go along with them. For a while it's good fun to hold on just to see if you can do it. Sometimes it kind of feels good to get a full swollen feeling in the bottom. You can get this by holding on to the poos. But mainly we hold because it's a way of beating our parents at their own game. That is, a game of being boss. After all, there are two main holes we can open and shut. Our mouth and the other one. Both of these have important things passing through them. Food and poos are important not only to us, but also to our parents. It's one way of getting control of ourselves by learning to open and shut these holes when we want to, not just when our parents want us to.

It is kind of interesting to see what our parents will do if we should hold on to our poos for a while. Some parents are not anxious about it and they just don't take any notice. So after a while we find it very unpleasant to have all our poos inside us and push it out. Soon we learn not to hold it in because the only one it hurts is ourselves. But some of our parents are pretty anxious so they try to force our poos out of us. They might do this in any way that seems to work for them. To us some of these ways just don't make sense. If parents (and that includes chemists, who are usually parents as well) thought as logically as we do, they would also see that some methods don't make sense. To get us to use our bowels all they need to do is feed us food and fluids, give us plenty of attention and some activity and forget about our bowels. Their pushing things into our bottom (even if they are all greasy, they still hurt), or foul tasting stuff in our mouths, is really over doing it. They might have a temporary victory, but in the long run we will win. If they want us to turn out like all those neurotic old ladies who spend fortunes at the chemist for different kinds of stuff to make them do poos properly, our parents just need to be real anxious over our bowels and try to push our poos out of us.

Sometimes we get to having diarrhoea. This is for most people almost as bad as vomiting. Usually as babies we get diarrhoea because we get an infection in our bowel, or because we get too much fatty food, or our parents like lots of onions and expect us to like them too. Just like most people would not vomit if they could help it so would very few want to have diarrhoea. There are a few of us who might not like the idea of diarrhoea for themselves but kind of enjoy having it because of the effect it has on others. When we are babies or just toddlers we notice if we should have diarrhoea that awful look people get on their faces. We also notice how they screw up their noses and kind of get angry with anyone who has diarrhoea. So we learn to connect diarrhoea with an angry bad thing to do. Also we get loose runny poos if we get a bit excited. This seems to happen to most of us at some time or other. If these things happen very often and particularly if we have parents who are against doing poos, who are very clean and tidy, neat and exact and very often angry without showing it openly, we become aware of a general idea. We learn that having diarrhoea can be a way of getting rid of angry bad feelings. This happens very early in our lives. If it happens often we might even get a sickness called colitis, after a few years.

So there can be a number of bad things that come out of messing around with our poos and the way we do it. It's hard to teach our parents how to handle our poos especially if their parents have taught them lots of bad things. Still, we have to start somewhere. If only our parents could throw away their rules about toilet training we'd be a lot happier. This business of getting trained to do poos and wees is about as mixed up a subject as any that has anything to do with bringing us up. The rules that parents use are at times so odd, and at other times so rigid, and at times so cruel that I could almost write a book about just rules for when to, how to and where to do poos. There are no good rules. If there were, everyone would stick to them. Potting at three weeks of age and holding out when we are four years old are extremes. There are lots of stages in between.

If we are mainly left alone, set good examples by our parents and encouraged to do poos when we feel the urge we turn out all right. By the time we are two to three years old we really know what doing poos is all about. It might be a bit of a joke, something to whisper about, but we mostly feel pretty good if we have done our poos properly.

How to manage your parents when you are sucking your thumb

Probably the most fascinating thing about thumb sucking is that not all children do it. This is difficult to understand because it is usually such a pleasant, soothing thing to do. Sucking is after all one of the earliest things that we learn to do and seems to be more or less automatic from the time we are born. You may have noticed that babies don't really discriminate between whether it's a nipple or a finger, they just suck away and seem very pleased to do it.

When we are babies of course we mostly suck on a nipple, whether it's our mother's or one of those mass-produced things that are usually much bigger than mother's, but are said to do the job just as well. Babies need to suck to keep alive. If they can't suck they can't feed properly and if they can't feed properly they don't put on weight and everybody becomes very anxious, especially the Sister in the Baby Health Centre. Some babies of course really can't suck, either because they are weak or because they have something wrong with their mouth or lips or sometimes because the nipple they get is too big or too little or a funny shape or other things like that.

But when everything is going all right there is nothing better than the feeling we get as babies when we are nestled in somebody's arms and sucking at a teat. It soothes us and fills us with good things and makes us feel secure and safe and warm and wanted. If babies have any of the difficulties that I have already mentioned, it seems to be a terrific handicap, and some of us who never seem to get enough pleasure when we are at this sucking stage always seem to be trying to return to it, to somehow or other become totally dependent on someone again and sometimes to try and fill ourselves up with things in an effort to recapture the goodness of that early period. That's probably why some adults drink and smoke such a lot.

But when we are children of course our parents don't really feel that we should be indulging in all those kinds of things; they only let us drink beer or smoke a cigarette as a sort of a joke. If we try to take it up seriously they get very cross indeed. Sometimes they let us smoke just to make us sick and I think that's a very dirty trick indeed.

When we are old enough to have stopped sucking at a nipple some of us start sucking our fingers or our thumbs. If parents watched closely they could see that we usually do this at times when we need comforting, or at times when we want to feel safe and secure again—when we are going to sleep, when we are afraid or puzzled.

Somehow our parents don't seem to see it that way and they feel that it is a kind of threat or attack on themselves. Some of them feel, and perhaps they are really right, that it's a sort of reflection on them. They feel that somehow or other they did not really feed us enough, and of course they always mean food, although any child can tell you that food is about the *least* important thing that it wants from its parents. Being loved, feeling safe and secure, is an important thing to all of us.

Sometimes of course sucking our thumb is a passing phase and when we get a little older and feel more secure and safe and confident we give it up. That is unless it's become a sort of a competition between our parents and ourselves to see who is going to win. When this happens there is no doubt that we have the upper hand, so to speak. Parents don't like other people to see their children sucking their thumbs and they will go to almost any length to pretend that it doesn't happen. We must be very careful when we do it and where we do it and we have to be tolerant of the fact that our parents are just confused and embarrassed by us putting our thumb in our mouth.

Then of course there is also what we could call 'fluffy blanket habit'. Mothers often call it 'that old rag' or if they get angry with us 'that dirty old rag'. It might be a blanket or sheet from our bassinet or cot, it might be a nappy or towel, it can be an old dress of ours or a piece of mother's dressing gown. Usually it's fluffy. Sometimes it's got to be so fluffy that it's only cotton wool or bits of cotton waste that will do. No matter what it is we usually do approximately the same thing with it. We hold it near our mouth and nose. Sometimes we suck it or chew it, sometimes we just brush it on our lips, sometimes we lick it. Mostly we sniff it or sniff and chew at the same time. Some of us get bits of it up our nose, even twiddling it in our fingers and putting it near our nose can be the same kind of thing to do.

How can all these kind of connect, these different things be the same? They aren't, but there is always something basic to all of them. This thing we use has a special meaning for us. Special meanings might change, but there is always something special about it. Mainly it's a way of making us get used to the idea that even if mother is not there we'll still be all right. The special meaning might then be that our fluffy blanket, or whatever it is, is the same as mother, or may be by sniffing at the blanket we are pretending we can get the smell of mother close to us, even inside us, and that smell will make us so close to mother it will be the same as being with her.

It's this being the same as mother that is very important to us, especially when we are about seven or eight or nine or ten months old. Before then we kind of know we are the same as her because we can't really tell the difference between us. Then when we start to be able to do this, to see that other people are separate from ourselves, then we get into this habit, the fluffy blanket habit. It's the frightening feeling of being separate that makes us try to stay the same as, close to, and tied up with mother. As we realise we can't be, so we find a kind of substitute. This is our fluffy blanket.

Now this substitute we need for either a long time or sometimes for a short time. It depends on how secure we feel in ourselves, as to when we give it up. If we grow up in a happy, secure kind of home we might only need our fluffy blanket habit for a few months. If we hang on to it till we are three or four years old, or even older, it's because we need it. I can't think of any child I know who had a blanket and didn't still need it. Blankets get thrown away at times by children and at other times parents get rid of them. They only get removed by us or our parents, if we have grown up enough to do without them. This growing up really means being independent enough, not having to be frightened of being separate from and so not able to depend on, mother.

Sometimes we do hang on to our blankets longer than we need them for a security reason. Maybe mother has tried to keep us a baby for too long and our blanket is a thing she really insists on us having (like a bottle is sometimes forced on us by our mothers, even if we don't want it). If this has happened and we are then forced to give up our blanket we don't usually mind, but if we still need our blanket for the original reasons we started with it, then we are likely to feel a bit down in the dumps if it gets taken away from us. It's like losing an old friend (or, even more true to say, like losing our oldest friend—mother).

There are some children who never ever have a fluffy blanket and never want one. Some of these are normal and healthy—most are not. Before we can want to find a substitute for mother we have to feel that mother is important to us. Some of us never get the chance to feel that, if we never had a mother who looked after us, because we are what's called an orphan, or because our mother left us, or because she died and then we lived in a place where children who don't have mothers live. We mightn't have had the chance of finding someone else to latch on to and use instead of a mother. Others of us have a mother, but she is not really keen on the job of being mother, might even hate us and even might try to get rid of us. Still others have mothers who really do love us, but who themselves get very down in the dumps and can't think or feel enough about us for us to feel good about their being with us, for us to feel that they are important to us.

Fluffy teddy bears and other toys are a bit like fluffy blankets. They might do exactly the same job for us. If we remember all the things about fluffy blankets we could say exactly the same about teddy bears. There are some other things to say as well. Teddy bears and all kinds of not quite real looking animals are important parts of our parents' equipment. They belong to us but they are mostly part of our parents' equipment. Parents (or parent pretenders like aunts and grandmothers) give them to us. We chose our own fluffy blankets, but parents give us our teddy bears. They give them to us often because they love us and want to give us a gift of their love, but sometimes I feel they might not love us enough and want to make sure we really don't know that, or they would be embarrassed or ashamed or guilty. So they give us teddy bears as a proof of their love. Then you might get a very big teddy bear if they need to prove their love very much, but only a little teddy bear if they are pretty confident in their love for you. It might even be that instead of feeling guilty about not loving you enough your parents don't really love you very much at all, that they only want to keep up appearances, so they give you teddy bears and so on, because they hear it is the done thing to do.

So teddy might become important to you as a substitute or reminder of mother. More often it becomes a way of making yourself feel good—a pacifier. Parents often start this off as well. When they are angry with you and you cry and they won't pick you up then they give you teddy to to hang on to, instead of hanging on to them. After a while you get used this idea and every time you get growled at you grab for teddy and make yourself feel good again. It might not be your parents' fault, it might not be anybody's fault, it just might be a kind of accident that teddy or golliwog or rabbit gets used to pacify you. But if it is to become a real good pacifier it has to look, to you at least, a bit like mother or father.

Whether we suck our thumbs, a blanket or teddy's ears, it seems that when we are babies parents always want us to grow up. They can never wait until we sit up or crawl or stand up or walk. When we say our first words they go into ecstasies and bore all the other parents by talking about how quick and clever we are. However, as soon as they perceive that we are really growing up they want us to be like babies again, and cuddle and kiss us, long after we want them to, and treat us like babies, long after they ought to. But there is one thing that they can't stand, and that is when we are no longer babies and we persist in acting like one. Parents become angry and don't seem to understand how strong our need is sometimes so that we will suck away until sometimes we even hurt our teeth or our thumbs. They don't seem to know that they can't just take this nice feeling away from us, without replacing it with something just as good or better.

A favourite saying of parents is 'Don't be a baby.' They just don't seem to understand that that's exactly what we want to be sometimes. Instead they make fun of us, punish us, dress us in babies' clothes, put us back into nappies or put mustard on our thumbs. Sometimes they even tie up not only our thumbs but our whole hand. Worse still they might take away our pacifier or teddy.

They just don't seem to get the idea that what we want to do is grow up in our own way, at our own pace, and that they can help us best by not fighting us about our blankets or our thumbs, but by giving us secure love instead.

In the end, however, they can't really win because we can always get our own back by showing them exactly how grown up we have become; we stop sucking our thumb and start masturbating.[1]

How to educate your parents about rocking and rolling

Rocking comes naturally to all of us. Maybe it starts when we are real small and get rocked in our mother's arms. You hear of this being a good way of getting a baby to sleep. Sometimes it seems to make mother go to sleep too. But it feels real nice and often gets to be so nice we yell as soon as mother stops rocking us. I suppose it must be annoying for grown ups to stand with a baby in their arms and rock back and forth for a long time, then to twist and contort themselves around so as to see if baby's eyes are shut and find they are open and looking straight at them. It's probably even more annoying when rocking has stopped

[1] See *How to handle your parents when they discover you have been masturbating.*

us from crying and as soon as we notice that the rocking has stopped our crying starts again. This crying kind of shows just how much we like rocking movements.

Rocking always starts with someone else, usually mother, providing the motor power. To do that she has to get pretty close to us, either holding us or at least standing real close to our cot or bassinet. So maybe it isn't just the rocking movement by itself, but also the being close to someone, that makes it nice. Anyway, after a while we learn how to turn on this motor ourselves and we can move parts of ourselves around, and as we get bigger rock our whole bodies around. We all do it; I have never heard of babies that did not rock, even if they only did it for a few times and for a few minutes. So it's not the rocking itself that is disturbing to parents but how long you do it for and when you do it.

After a while rocking gets used to make us feel good whenever we reckon we need it. It might be that we feel lonely because no-one is around, or worse still there are plenty of people around but we don't seem to be able to get close to people. This is one of the secrets, this getting close to people, that no-one really teaches us. Some of us have got it, some haven't. Rocking might also get used if we feel hurt in our body or in our feelings, or if we feel bad. If we get real frightened, it might be worth while trying it. Disturbed rocking, the kind of rocking that disturbs our parents, never happens when we are feeling good. They soon catch on, they get the feeling that we are rocking to get rid of a bad feeling; it's almost as if we kind of rock off the bad feeling and pass it on to them. Almost all of them get angry if we rock and they might not know that they are angry, but even if they distract us by offering anything from an ice cream to a new teddy bear, it's really only to make themselves feel better about us and less angry. Rocking is one thing that parents can't ignore, because when we really get into the swing of it, it's kind of possible to wreck furniture, make holes in walls and wear out the carpets on the floor, not to say anything of all the squeaking and scratching and banging noises we can make with it. Adults don't feel good about us rocking, it makes them real uncomfortable. The more they try to stop us the more we do it.

It's true as we get bigger that the way we rock changes. At first it might just be rocking back and forth on our tummies, then on our knees and then on all fours. Later we can rock sitting up, standing, leaning or lying down. So it's real hard to be a parent of a child who rocks. Really we've got to feel sympathy for them, but only if they recognise that rocking is not a bad thing, but a distress signal. If we rock a lot we need help. We are trying to give ourselves this help through rocking.

Rolling is very much the same as rocking, only it's much less common and usually it's only for the young. It also starts when we are real small, usually by experimenting with our bodies to see what we can make ourselves do. Then rolling might get to be a way of feeling good. It could even get to be a way of getting rid of bad feelings, only it usually turns into a way of getting somewhere, of moving around. With lots of habits like this, if they can be made to serve a useful purpose they get used. After a while we learn to crawl, walk and so on, and so rolling gets taken off our list of tricks. We can see how important it must have been to some of us, because it comes back at different times as we grow up. When we are about four or five or even nine or ten it's fun to roll down hills, especially if they're dirty ones. Some adults roll around in barrels, even over waterfalls, which wouldn't be our idea of fun. Other grown ups use rolling in its original form. They roll around and feel good, only now they don't do it by themselves, they usually hang on to someone else while they roll.

Head banging is a bit different from rocking and rolling. Head banging seems to everyone that sees it a pretty way out thing to do. It is. To a tiny baby it might make sense, but not to us when we grow up a bit. That's why tiny babies are usually the only ones to do it, but sometimes older children and even grown up children do it. Then they are really just being like babies. There seems to be quite a number of places to bang your head on. The earliest one is the end of the bassinet, or you can try banging it on mum's chest, or even on her head if you can get near it. Sometimes it's only the kitchen table when you get washed and sometimes it's the floor when you're allowed to get on it. The amazing thing about all these places is that none of them is soft, so head banging must hurt. One of the things about head banging is that it goes on and on and then you hear mother and father say, 'You'd think it would hurt him, but he seems to like it.'

No baby really does like it. To us, when we are babies, head banging is better than nothing. That is, usually we bang our heads if we are frustrated because we are not able to move around enough, like by being kept in our cots for a long time each day. We might get frustrated because there is something wrong with our way of moving around, because our muscles might not work properly or our nerves not do their job. So we bang our heads to kind of get rid of feelings of being tense.

But most often we bang our heads when we feel that no-one loves us or cares about us. This might be true; parents might feel love for us, but that's not the way we see it. Maybe our parents only spend a short time with us or they growl a lot or are pretty tense themselves.

Nodding is another thing that makes us feel good. You can tell we feel good because we get our far away look on our faces, the same look grown ups get if they drink a lot of wine or read a book or maybe when they think secret thoughts. It's a good thing we can't always tell what their secret thoughts are because our parents might get cross if we found out. Just the same they don't give us credit for having our own special thoughts. These might be all about what it feels like when we get cuddled or what it's like wrapped up asleep in our nice warm cots or even floating around in the bath or some other luxury. Nodding seems to make it easier to remember.

There is another habit that most of us like, but very few of us keep up for very long. It's called whirling. Whirling is exciting, it's a kind of dance without rules. The main thing about it is that it's a way of getting a lot of feeling out of us. If we whirl and whirl we kind of lose our balance. Grown ups say that people who lose their balance are mad. It might be better to say that we lose control of ourselves. It seems all right to do that, to giggle and fall over and squirm and nearly get sick, to kind of feel excited and frightened at the same time. But it's only all right if you are young and also if you can stop it if you want to. All of us like our fathers or any other long suffering man who is prepared to whirl us, to do it for us sometimes. It's nice to be big enough to do it for ourselves, but I've got to agree with grown ups that it's kind of mad to keep on doing it over and over again. Those of us who do it probably need to get some help to get over it.

Sniffing used to be a very popular thing for grown ups to do. In the olden days, they used to have a snuff box, usually with jewels on it and they loved making loud sniffing noises. We sniff all the time, but usually our parents are so sophisticated or maybe they can't afford to give us jewelled snuff boxes, so they get at us to stop sniffing. Maybe they forget that it's easier to sniff than to blow your nose. It's really a hard trick to get hold of, this business of using a handkerchief, of squeezing your nose and blowing at the same time. After all, it hurts in the ears and they go pop which is not the most pleasant of feelings. If blowing out is supposed to get rid of all that stuff that blocks our nose, why shouldn't sniffing do the same thing?

It isn't only nose blowing that makes us sniff. Sometimes if we are a bit frightened of not being able to breathe properly, like after we've had a few swimming lessons we might start to sniff. Our swimming teachers (only they have to pretend they're not teachers but a thing called an instructor) usually insist that the best way to learn to swim is to pretend to be a fish and put our heads under water. They don't realise that we can't breathe under water. Most of them are pretty much like real fish, so I suppose they can breathe under water, but we can't. Being good, obedient children we want to do what our parents say. We have to learn to swim. Just the same, it's always a bit doubtful whether once you get your head under water you will ever come up again and be able to breathe properly. To keep on reminding ourselves that we still can breathe air and not water we keep on sniffing.

There is no doubt that we can get up to lots of tricks like this that will really upset our parents. Some of the time of course we know this and we do it anyway. But most of the time the things we do are not just crazy or irritating or bad or ugly, they also mean something and usually it is something very important, to us anyway. Even though we get a lot of satisfaction out of all of these things that we do, there isn't too much doubt that most of us would give them up without thinking twice if we felt we were going to get something better to replace them. But of course that can only be more and more of our parents' love and affection and time, and sometimes that seems to be too much to expect.

NOW WE ARE
TODDLING

How to cope with your parents if you can't keep still

As a general rule parents don't like restless children. They like us to be very quiet, and to speak when we are spoken to, and to be seen but not heard, and if possible not to be seen too often either. A lot of parents who have children are surprised to find out that they make noises and smells and demands on their time, far worse than any cat or dog could do. After a while, of course, most parents seem to resign themselves to the unhappy facts and more or less cope with them.

However, things start to get a bit difficult if they get landed with what is now fashionably called 'a hyperkinetic child'. I think hyperkinetic means more or less lots of energy which isn't really such a bad thing, but the way the term is used by parents and some doctors, it's more like a swear word. Parents love to be able to say, 'He is such a good baby, you would hardly know he was there.' So that when things turn out the opposite they often try for a while to make it all seem all right by making up lots of stories that nobody else ever really believes. Things like 'He is just high spirited,' or 'Boys will be boys.' Of course this is a bit of a problem if it happens to be a girl, but then, interestingly enough, restless, overactive children mostly seem to be of the male sex.

After a few months or sometimes as much as a few years, most parents seem to crack under the pressure and then we have to watch out for trouble. They start off by trying to shame us into being better behaved. 'You are a big boy now and should be able to sit still at the table', or 'Bobby next door is younger than you, he is always well behaved and never spills his food on the table,' which of course makes us hate Bobby next door like anything. And then they usually try bribery. Parents never seem to lose their surprise at the fact that bribery works. Their surprise at this is only exceeded by their surprise when they find out that it doesn't always work, and that eventually it stops working altogether. Their attitude to bribery is really a little difficult to understand, especially when you realise as you get older that most adults accept bribes, but usually only when no-one is looking. Those of them who are never lucky enough to be offered a bribe are the only ones who seem to say that they would never accept one.

When the bribe stops working then they lose their tempers. It is often at this stage that your neighbours and your grandparents and perhaps even your doctor will be brought into it. 'I have tried everything with him, being nice to him, and understanding, and patient, and even belting him, but nothing works.' The reasons why nothing works are really very simple, as you know. It seems to me that it is because of one of two reasons. Either we really can't help it or else our parents really don't want us to stop it.

It is an interesting fact that some of us are just born restless. We don't seem to be able to sit, stop, look and listen with the rest of you. We are always restless and active and we can't concentrate on anything for very long. We are always being what grown ups call 'naughty'. We never seem to do what we are told, although often we start to do it. We never seem really to learn what we are taught although we often half learn it. It's not so much that we are disobedient as that we don't really seem to comprehend what is required of us. Sometimes when we really put on a terrific effort we seem to improve a little, but it often takes a long time, sometimes years, before we really find that we are able to control our movements and our behaviour and concentration the way most children do. Being like this is bad enough, but the whole thing becomes intolerable when we find ourselves in the situation where our parents don't seem to understand this, and keep treating us as if we will be able to stop things if only they can hit on the right inducement for us to do so. That's why we get all the psychological warfare, which ends up in frustration and anger and resentment and depression for them and us. Of course we have to understand that parents are entitled to set some kind of standards for their children. It's no good saying, 'Oh, I just can't help it, so you will have to put up with me being a little pig.' I think it's pretty reasonable of them to expect us to keep up some sort of standard, and to keep showing us what they want us to do and how they want us to behave. But it gets very difficult to cope if they are not even willing to meet us half way on this.

The other problem of course is even worse. This is where it is highly unlikely that our parents really want us to be 'sweet little things' at all, where often the opposite seems to be the case. One or other of them keeps provoking us and needling us and pushing us until we are so confused that we don't know how to behave at all. Often we can see what is going on around us and it makes us very worried indeed. There seem to be all sorts of feelings inside our parents, often that they don't understand or realise or acknowledge even to themselves. They seem to want us to be bad and to want us to be naughty and even destructive. It's almost as if they need to have a bad part of themselves to threaten and control and sometimes even to beat as long as that bad part seems to be in us and not in them. Once they start us off in this way we often can't stop. In the end they might realise that the badness that they see in us is only a reflection of themselves and then they become very depressed indeed.

Although it will be difficult for them, the kind of thing that they can do best for us is to be patient. To accept us as we are and not as the bad version of what they had fondly hoped we might have been. Their 'little darling'. Nowadays it is often possible for parents to settle us down by giving us a tranquilliser or something like that. I am not against that at all, and I think that sometimes it is helpful to be made to feel calmer and quieter and it is often the beginning of a very wonderful friendship with our family that we never thought possible. But it is always a great disappointment when parents become like many doctors and begin giving you a pill instead of giving you understanding.

How to handle your parents when you are having a temper tantrum

It might be better if I had called this chapter 'How to handle your parents when they don't know how to handle your temper tantrum', because this is probably the biggest problem involved here. Temper tantrums themselves aren't so bad or so frightening, the trouble really starts when your parents don't seem to know what to do about them. It can be a very frightening thing to find that you have lost control, but it is even more frightening to find that your parents have lost control as well.

We all know temper tantrums are very common. Most of us have them at some stage or another, although it's more common when we are younger than five. This is probably because we have less ways of expressing ourselves then, so if we really want to make a point or to let people know how we feel, it's got to be done dramatically. Another reason of course is that when we are young we see things pretty much as black and white. Things are good and bad, reassuring or frightening, totally interesting or a bore. But one thing is pretty certain: when we decide we want something, or that we want to do something, we want it now. (In fact, now is not soon enough.) If we can't, a lot of us have a temper tantrum. It's obvious to most people, but if your parents are anxious, they may not see it. They may think that there are all sorts of other reasons for you behaving in this, to them, very disturbing manner. Sometimes they think you are sick and sometimes they even think you are mad.

As we get older, of course, the sort of temper tantrums we have become much more sophisticated. You may not believe it, but even adults have tantrums when they are frustrated with each other, and even more incredibly, parents sometimes have tantrums in front of their children. They do this in all sorts of ways. Sometimes they break things. Sometimes, and this is always much more frightening if you are watching, they throw things at each other or even hit each other. But the most effective way apparently is just not to talk to whoever they are angry with. This is something that you have to be very careful to do well and I would not recommend it for children, although they sometimes try it.

There are various kinds of temper tantrums. For example there are the floor banging, door banging and cup or saucer banging type: and then there are the brother or sister bashing, parent bashing or even self bashing type. Added to this there is the often screaming type, and probably the most effective that any of us can use is the breath holding type. In this one you have to hold your breath, often until you are blue in the face, and this is a very frightening sight indeed. Unfortunately this kind of tantrum can often get out of hand. When this happens you may have to be turned upside down and slapped very hard on the back to get you breathing again. Although this can be a little bit humiliating because it is so much like being a new-born baby, it often brings with it a lot of concern and cuddling from your parents. By this time you probably can't remember why you had the tantrum in the first place and your parents are so glad that you are all right that you will get anything you want anyway.

Although tantrums are really to get what we want when we want it, we have tantrums for various sorts of reasons. Often in the beginning it is just to attract attention and in many cases I am sure we would never repeat it more than once or twice, if it wasn't for the fact that some parents seem to encourage us. You have probably heard them all say at one time or another, 'Isn't she just adorable?' and then they can't seem to understand why we keep doing it. Because most of them refuse to remember what they were like when they were children, they keep encouraging us until all of a sudden our temper tantrums begin to become an embarrassment to them. This is a crucial period because it is now that we first realise what a valuable weapon we have. Sometimes we can get all sorts of things from our parents, not just attention, but things to eat, watching T.V., staying up late, going out to play and sometimes not going to school. Probably the best result that a boy can hope for when he has a tantrum is that he will split up his parents, especially if he finds his mother is on his side and she starts calling his father things like 'aggressive, unfeeling beast'. Once again though there is a bit of a problem—the whole situation might backfire on us. This is because once we start a tantrum, we often don't know how to control it, and if we lose control there is a very good chance that we may undo all of the things that we need so badly from our parents, especially their confidence in themselves and in the way that they handle us. We can make our mothers feel very inadequate and often depressed and when this happens we often get depressed ourselves.

Like most troubles we get caught up in, having tantrums is one that worries our parents much more than it does us. It's when they get so worried they don't know what to do that we'd like to give them some advice on how to handle us. If they would stay calm and in control and not give in to us we'd pretty often get the message that tantrums are not really any use, except to let out our feelings. Mostly there are better ways of doing that, so if we get frustrated by not finding any benefits coming to us from our tantrums, we'll find ourselves having to let our feelings be known in more grown up ways and asking for things by talking instead of screaming. But most of all we might even learn that we can wait till tomorrow to get what we want, especially if tomorrow comes pretty soon. But if you really need something from your parents or if you really want to test them out to see how mature and adequate they are, a tantrum is a pretty quick way to do it. It may not be a fair way, because anything that embarrasses or frightens or attacks other people is likely to take unfair advantage of certain aspects of them that they can't really do a great deal about. But if you are only doing it in self defence, then I suppose it is all right. After all, if our parents make us feel safe and control us fairly but firmly, a tantrum or two isn't really going to worry them, and it will make us feel a lot better. Especially after it's over.

How to bring up your parents when the new baby arrives

When your parents' next offspring comes along you will probably have (or will have had) a mixture of feelings. Your interest in the baby will fight with your wish that there was really no new baby. You will probably love, want to cuddle, look after, fetch and carry for it and at the same time feel like scratching, biting, tipping it out of its basket or throwing dirt over this newcomer. At this time most of us feel pretty put out and say to ourselves, 'What's that woman done to me now, I'm her baby, why does she need another one?' Your anger towards the baby is really exceeded by your angry feelings for mum (but whoever heard of a little boy or girl being angry with their mother?). Sometimes it's easier to become mummy's little angel by doing everything just right. You show her how much you love her and the baby, just so she can't see how your 'bad' feelings of dislike and even hate are really churning you up.

Parents like to believe that their children look forward to having a brother or sister and if you disillusion them by being nasty and showing them how you really feel, they get angry themselves. They might say, 'I brought the baby home especially for you, so I don't know why you are so ungrateful,' or, more directly, 'If you can't be nice to your little brother I will send you back where he came from,' or even 'If I catch you hurting Johnny again I will get the doctor to take you away in his black bag.' So to make sure that mum and dad still like you it's kind of necessary to pretend that you are even better than you are. This plan sometimes misfires, because Mums and Dads then say, often to their own parents, 'See how well he has taken to the baby, it hasn't disturbed him at all,' or 'It's so sweet to see her being nice to her little sister, she really must love her.' This pleases them a lot and they are happy to forget about you because you are not showing any feelings that upset them. When they seem to forget you (not altogether, just enough to make it hurt), you probably feel that there must be something you can do to get a bit more attention.

Being good was pretty hard and didn't pay dividends, so we try the other side of human nature now by really laying it on—having tantrums, demanding food, breaking toys, screaming at night, or any of those other tricks you found to work for you before—you try to win back mum and sometimes even dad. Even this is not enough for some parents, so more direct action is needed—you fill your pants while mum is feeding the baby, or paint her kitchen with jam and flour when baby is in the bath. To this most parents will respond as you expect them to, getting real mad and hitting out. You can always console yourself by saying that this kind of attention is better than none. If by chance your parents show far less than average response to your behaviour you might need to pull out all the stops by hurting your baby brother or sister. If all else fails you might even wee into your brother's cot to set the seal on your disapproval.

Of course, the troubles we have in educating our parents when the baby arrives really started long before this. For some months you have known that there is something different about mum, she has been vomiting her breakfast and occasionally all her meals. To confuse the situation somewhat dad may have had the same symptoms. Though your parents don't know it, you are pretty perceptive. The changes of mum's bustline, the filling out of her face and the eventual change in her figure (even if she pretends that this year's fashion is rather fuller in line than the previous years) haven't escaped your keen gaze. If you comment on these changes you are likely to be told that it is none of your business, you are not old enough to understand, or to go and play and stop annoying mum. At times you try to prove to yourself that your eyes did not deceive you, by punching Mum in the chest or hugging her a bit tighter, just to feel what is really going on. If you feel your guess is correct and you apparently by chance say, 'I want you to have another baby,' or 'I'd love to have a baby brother or sister,' just to test mum's response, you don't have to be too quick to notice her blush or her excessive anger with you. It's better still to try it out on Dad, because he probably feels more embarrassed by the whole proceeding and is more likely to over-react to your remark. By pursuing this tactic you may be lucky enough to be told that soon you will have a baby brother or sister, that mum is going to go to the doctor and he will give her a new baby, or that when she comes back from hospital she will bring a baby with her.

This kind of explanation will satisfy most parents that now they have done their duty and prepared you for the happy event. However, when you ask yourselves when, where, why and how all this is going to come about, the answers you come up with are not likely to satisfy you. If you try really hard you might annoy your parents enough for them to sit down and explain that babies are carried in mum's tummy, that God puts a seed next to mummy's heart and that it grows there, or even more obscurely that just like the baker bakes his buns so does mother cook the baby inside her. All these answers probably fill you with funny feelings—adults call some of these anxiety, or if you are old enough guilt, shame, doubt, envy and lots of other names too hard for us to understand. Being pretty practical you will probably wonder what's going to happen to you while the doctor is doing his job in the hospital looking after mum; who is going to look after you? Most likely you will feel pretty insecure and sometimes already anticipate that mum, if she is going to be away from home, might not even come back. Because while we are young most of the things we need to make us happy come from mum, we might often start to consider the possibility of losing out on these necessary things and get a bit sad, but over and above all this, those 'bad' feelings we mentioned before will sometimes start to make their presence felt in all kinds of odd ways. Just as mummy vomits so might you, as her tummy gets bigger your tummy might start to hurt, and just by chance those nice drawings you did for your kindergarten teacher turn all messy. If you are a girl and at the age when dolls are your confidants you might spend a lot of time whispering to them. Boys are not usually lucky enough to be allowed by their parents to play with dolls, because it is not manly, so they could well start painting people with big abdomens or fill up their dump trucks or car carriers with lots of little cars, or even better still with mud from the vegetable garden.

Eventually the day arrives (or, as is popularly thought to be always the case, a night) and with what seems like unnecessary haste and confusion mum is escorted out of the home by dad. Between a few hours and days later dad will come up to you and proudly announce that you have got a new brother or sister, sometimes he might even tell you that your baby has been born. Now most of you will already have worked this out by yourselves. Grandmothers are also a pretty reliable source of information in this area and if your favourite Nanna has been looking after you she will probably have whispered into your ear the secret that has been kept from you all this time. Most of us will immediately feel that we would like to rush off to hospital and see the baby—and mum. There are some children who have really been kept in the dark and they find this information hard to handle—sometimes so hard that they go into a state of shock, stop talking, just sit and stare into space, or perhaps curl up in a corner and whimper. These days some hospitals have become enlightened enough to realise that mums have other children and have opened the doors of the maternity section so that children can visit their mothers in hospital. But for the majority of us the crucial test will come when mum brings baby home. The way we feel is sort of like how mummy would feel if one Daddy day arrived on the doorstep with a new young beautiful girl. 'She is going to live with us,' he would say. 'I love her very much, but of course I still love you.'

If you have not seen mum for a week or so you might not seem to recognise her. It's better not to do this because parents place great store by us rushing up to mum as if nothing has happened and saying something endearing, even if somewhat incongruous, like 'What's for tea?' If you are pretty stunned by the new appearance of mum because by this time you'd pretty well decided that she had gone away for good, even died, it is very hard to be spontaneous and it's easier for you to say nothing. If you still find it hard to speak after a few days your parents will probably recognise your distress. Perhaps it is better to straight away compete with the baby by wetting your bed, talking what parents call baby talk, stopping eating, going back to sucking a dummy and, if there are none left, your thumb, or any similar manoeuvres to let your parents know that you have had quite a shock. But it isn't really necessary for us to be shocked or our parents to be angry or depressed. Having brothers or sisters is often inevitable and sometimes it even turns out to be a good thing. What we need though is for our parents to understand our side of things, to give us more of themselves than they think we need and to be patient. It takes a while, to get used to being out of the central spotlight and it's not really unreasonable to expect some sort of compensation. The interesting thing is that the first time always seems to be the worst (provided it doesn't happen too often).

After the first few days the difficult job you and your whole family have in learning to live a new way of life is under way. Your task is to accept the baby and show it, mum, and dad, and anybody else who is interested, that even though you feel 'bad' about some aspects of this new life you also really love it. To like to be in a house full of nappies and night feeds, dummies and dozens of sterilised bottles, a mum who is alternately elated and so tired that she cannot talk to you and a Dad who comes home to 'coo over the baby' instead of you, is a pretty hard lesson to learn. Yet it always seems to be a pretty big surprise to parents when their children get upset at this 'event'. You should not really let them down in their expectations of your goodness, but you will feel better if you do.

What to do with your parents when they put you in hospital

One thing you've got to know right from the beginning is that going into hospital is awful. I understand that some adults go into hospital at times 'for a rest'. When someone has to go to a place that is full of coughs and sneezes and funny noises and rather odd, unusual but terribly efficient, officious people, for a rest, then it must really be terrible at home. Another thing that I should warn you about, if you haven't already fallen into this trap, is to take absolutely no notice of all the talk that parents give you about all the nice things that happen to you when you are in hospital. Presents and things like that, and especially ice cream when you have your tonsils out. You can get terribly sick even of ice cream when you can't eat anything else because your throat hurts you so much.

Quite apart from whatever it is that you're going into hospital for, most of the problems for us are because of the way our parents and other adults go about it all. It wasn't until fairly recently that they realised how badly we feel about being separated from them. Even when they accepted this fact they still couldn't believe that the younger we were the more we missed them. You still hear lots of them say, 'Oh, he's only a baby, he's too young to know what's going on.' But when you have only lived a couple of months, a day is an awful long time, an hour is as long as a day, and a day doesn't really have any end at all. When we are little we don't know how to tell the time and when our parents leave us we are sure they are never coming back. What sometimes makes it worse is that often we feel they are not coming back because of something bad in us, or something bad that we have done, and this can make us very upset indeed.

It seems very strange to me that parents never seem to realise that meeting new people and going to strange places is in any way upsetting to children. If you have ever been in hospital you will know the sort of things I mean. It usually all starts in the morning when our mothers or our fathers or both come in with a big smile and say, 'Aren't you lucky? Today is the day that you are going into hospital.' Now if they have done a very good job of brain washing, they will have managed to tell you some fairy story about the nice things that will happen to you there, and for a while you might even believe them. Some of them may have been playing doctors and nurses with you for weeks, so that you won't be frightened by white coats or by injections or stethoscopes or things like that. You get dressed in a hurry and your mother is often so busy seeing that she has packed all the things that the hospital gave her in a big list that she might forget to put in your favourite doll or your favourite blanket or whatever it is you like to suck or cuddle up to when you are going to sleep. Sometimes you will not remind her about this because it has never entered your head that you are actually going to sleep in this new place.

Sometimes if they have been really cowardly, as they often are, they will pretend to you that you are just going for a drive or to the playground, and then all of a sudden they pull up in front of this great big building with lots of windows that somehow always manage to look frightening. You still probably haven't quite caught on to what is going to happen so you walk inside. Mummy takes you up to a desk where the first thing that happens is that a lady smiles at you and asks you what your name is. She writes some things down on a sheet of paper and then she usually asks a man whom they call an orderly to take you to some other place. While you are on the way there he usually smiles at you and asks you what your name is. After a while you usually meet two or three other people who keep smiling at you and then eventually you go into what they call a ward. Here there is usually a lady in charge who you have to call Sister, although she is of course no relation to you whatsoever. This Sister smiles at you and asks you what your name is and then calls over another younger woman who is called a nurse. She takes you and your mummy and sits you down and makes a list of all the things that you have brought with you. She is usually friendlier than most, but by this time you are pretty sick of people smiling at you and asking you what your name is, and besides that you are probably starting to get a bit anxious at this time.

What happens from this point on varies a bit. In some of the hospitals they seem to have found out that children and particularly young children get terribly upset if they are separated from their mummies, so they let the mummies stay, and sometimes even in the same room. Unfortunately these places seem to be pretty rare and even though most children's doctors agree about this nowadays, not many of them seem to do much to make sure that you won't be separated from your mummy. So mostly about this time your mummy will say goodbye to you. For some of us this will of course be the first time she has ever said goodbye and we don't really understand what it means, but we pretty soon find out. All of a sudden our clothes are taken off us, we are put in a bath, we usually have a funny sort of white nightdress put on us and they shove us in a sort of a cot which has got iron bars all around us just like a cage in the zoo. It isn't until all this rush and bustle is over that we really have a good chance to look around at the place our parents have left us in.

It really is a strange place. All around you, you can see other children in other cages. Sometimes they will have plonked down next to you some toy that you have never seen before and which looks as if other people have used it. If we have brought something we know with us, we usually cling to it very tight. All around the room we can see children doing different things. Some are just sitting crying, some are sitting looking just as bewildered as we are, some seem to be playing all right although they don't really have much contact with anybody else. But the worst ones are the ones who just sit and don't move and don't speak and don't do anything. There seems to be something terribly hopeless and upsetting about them so we often don't look at them for very long. The interesting thing is that these kinds of different ways of feeling that children have in hospital don't seem to have anything to do with what they are in there for, it seems to be only to do with the fact that they are in there.

After the first little bit when we have got over feeling frightened and confused, we often begin to feel angry. Unfortunately there are not many ways that we can show how angry we are. One of them of course is at meal times and so we sometimes make it very hard indeed for those nice nurses to feed us. Sometimes if we feel that it upsets people around us we will cry a lot, but usually they don't take any notice. Our big opportunity really comes with the first time that mummy or daddy visits us. At first of course we are quite convinced that they have come to take us home and we will be very good indeed. We will laugh and smile at them and if we can speak we will say all sorts of nice things to them. After a while, however, we often begin to sense that something is wrong. Somehow or other they don't get very close to us. They may sit outside our cage and never even touch us. Sometimes if they do, they have a sort of a guilty look on their faces as if they are wondering whether they really should give us a cuddle or not. They usually bring us presents and after a while because we see that they are so embarrassed we spend most of the time looking at the presents they have brought us. We want to do everything we can to make sure that we don't upset them so that when they leave they will take us back home with them.

All of a sudden a very loud bell rings, something like a school bell, and then mummy and daddy get up and start to sort of edge away from you. Sometimes they will bend over and kiss you and if you cling to them they try to gradually ease you off as if you have some sort of catching disease. Slowly but surely they back away from your cage to the door and all the time they keep smiling at you, hoping that you don't sense that there is something very wrong. All of a sudden they are gone and you are finally having to face the fact that you are going to be in this place for good. This may be the first time that you cry, and the first time that you feel really deserted and depressed. Parents don't seem to understand that we have no way of knowing why we can't go home and for some funny reason they never seem to give us any hope that we will. We look at the presents they have brought us and play with them, somehow hoping that in some magic way this will bring them back to us. If we can look out of the window we might be lucky enough to see them driving away in their car or getting into a tram or bus and this leaves us with a little bit of hope that they might come back the same way. The next time that they visit, however, we are not quite so gay and happy and sometimes we even pretend that we don't notice that they are sitting next to us. Sometimes we might smile at them and they of course smile back, and in a way they seem almost relieved that we are not trying to get to them or to touch them or cuddle them. In a way probably they are a bit disappointed as well but they are frightened that if we get too close to them again we won't let them go. We usually spend the whole time looking as if we are really interested in what we are doing, looking through a book or playing with a toy, and we are often so good at this that mummy will say to daddy, 'I am so pleased he has settled in so well. He is not upset at all now.' What they don't know of course is that somehow or other we don't trust them quite so much and we are frightened each second that if we make a wrong move they will leave us. And sure enough they do.

It's at around this time that some of us who perhaps have never felt terribly secure or wanted or needed at home start to get really depressed. We don't talk much any more, we seem disinterested in everything, we don't play, we don't smile. This is the time when most of the nurses say to the doctors, 'They have settled in now and they are no trouble.' This is supposed to be a good thing, I think, but if only they knew how we really felt.

Fortunately for most of us we only have to stay for a short time and when the day comes when we are going it really is quite an experience. We can tell that there is something different right from the start because mummy or daddy or both walk in sort of confidently and gaily and they don't seem to worry any more about whether they pick us up. It is as if a great load has been lifted off them, but of course by this stage we are so suspicious that we just sit and bide our time. However, once we see our clothes and shoes we realise something good is going to happen and we can't get out of there fast enough. We grab mummy by the hand and pull her as hard as we can so that they usually say, 'Isn't he quaint?' It isn't until we are right out of that building and right back in our own home that we begin to relax a bit.

Of course sometimes, no matter how bad we feel, we just have to go into hospital, but you would think that someone would tell our parents about how we feel about it and that it is at times like these that we need the security and love we can get from them more than ever. The more we know about it all the less unhappy we will be and the longer we can be with them in hospital, the less unhappy we will become. If they are embarrassed and fearful over the whole business then we will be too. Sometimes they may even need to exaggerate all the lovings and kissings and cuddlings to help us cope with the strangeness and apparent danger of the situation we are in.

Of course once you are home your parents expect that everything is going to be just like it was before and that nothing will be changed. This just shows how little they really understand how we feel, so my advice to you is to do two things. First of all what you do is to pretend that they are not there. You don't kiss them and you don't cuddle them and if they come up to do it to you, you pretend you are still in that hospital and it really isn't allowed. This really upsets them and they get very depressed indeed. Then just as they are beginning to get frustrated and are dying to know what they can do to make you their 'little boy' or 'little girl' again, you rush up to them and kiss them and cuddle them until they can't take any more. They are so overjoyed to find that you still really love them that they will do anything at all for you and this is the time when you can really cash in. Most of us know this strategy and we become terribly demanding. We won't do anything that we don't like and we ask for all the things that we have been saving up to ask for, for months and months.

At first this works, but later on of course parents get pretty fed up with it. They begin to say things like, 'Ever since he has been to hospital he has become absolutely unreasonable and uncontrollable, I don't know what's come over him.' Or they'll say, 'If you don't settle down we'll put you back in hospital.' I suppose in some way we deserve to get told these things if we annoy them that much. But after all we have been through, why should they get off scot-free?

How to manage your parents if you talk funny

Before you can talk funny you have to be able to talk. It is quite hard to start to talk. Although only some mothers and fathers expect children to talk very early in their lives, most parents at some time or other wish that we had never started. Sometimes parents are quite sure that we have started to talk at the age of three or four months when we say 'mumma', 'dadda', 'bubba'. This is mainly because they are very keen for us to talk early so they can tell all their friends how clever they are to have such a clever child. It may sound like talking to them or they may pretend it's talking, or explain it as a kind of talking, but to us it's just good fun, practising moving our tongue and mouth or just doing what all babies are supposed to do. Anyhow even if you do make that noise on purpose you are not really old enough to know what it means. This is the main thing parents forget; they explain what we do as if we were adults just like themselves.

It is a different matter if some of us have not started to talk by the time we are eighteen months or so. There might be very good reasons for this. Probably there are always very good reasons, but somehow adults reckon some reasons are better than others. If you have not talked at all by this time you probably have noticed your parents doing all kinds of odd things. They will open and shut doors and sneak up behind you and make loud noises, clap hands and jingle money or keys at you. This is because nowadays most parents know that being deaf might be why you don't talk. If you are deaf it will be a pretty strange world you live in. One of the things that make it strange is that it is hard for you to understand why other people get angry with you and are irritated with you, or keep on doing things you don't want them to do for you. Because your parents or brothers and sisters use words to get things they want from each other and because you can't do this, you will probably feel pretty much out of things. Maybe you will be so much out of things that you reckon it is better for you to make your own kind of world and this is what your parents eventually recognise and call 'living in a world of your own'. Maybe for some of you who are deaf it gets to be a pretty frightening and frustrating kind of feeling. One way of letting other people know just how you feel is to get them real mad, by attacking them, breaking up your toys and their favourite things, or even by running away from home. This running away from home is usually called 'wandering', which seems more polite, because no parent would really like to believe that we would want to run away from them.

Some parents really make us not speak and also kind of run away from them. Not run away outside, but inside of us. This kind of means not getting too close to them. Usually we get close to our parents because they want us to, and one way of getting close is to talk with them. But these parents don't really like us to be children. They treat us more like machines that do things automatically at exact times and always by rules. When it comes to talking they try to make us talk very early, never let us talk like a baby should and insist on never ending practise, like over and over saying, 'Now, that's not right, say it again.' Eventually we feel we don't really want to get to tell these adults who happen to be our parents anything about ourselves, so we don't talk at all. If you are unlucky enough to have parents like this and you then meet other kinds of people you will get a big surprise, but not as big a surprise as your parents will when they hear of you talking quite freely to other people.

Many of us learn a different kind of talking. This is called gesture language. It's a thing we all do, but some of us do it better than others. This is often because we find it gets us everything we need and we don't have to bother to talk, we just point, or look, or screw up our faces in ways that make our parents say, 'Isn't she cute?', and give us what we want. Sometimes this kind of talking gets overdone, usually if parents reckon it's quicker for them if you do this than talk words or if you like being a baby perhaps because growing up has too many problems tied up with it.

Some mothers are especially good at stopping us from starting to talk. These are usually the kind who really go overboard if we make those cute gestures, but they also get over keen on their jobs as mothers. They do just everything for us, never let us learn how to feed ourselves or dress ourselves, or make sure that we don't get hurt, scared or upset and never, never, never leave us, even for a very short time. They are really 'too good' mothers. Just as they never let us do anything for ourselves, they also make it unnecessary for us to talk. It is a pretty hard thing to ever get away from this kind of mother and after a while you don't really want to. As time goes on you make sure you don't get away by not learning how to talk so other people can't understand you and so you have to depend on mother more and more. She makes it easier for you to do this because she always knows what you want. Sometimes it might get you confused because she seems to know what you want even before you yourself know what it is.

Not all mothers are like that, but for lots of different reasons quite a number of mothers find it hard to let us grow up. It may be because they find it easier having a baby than a bigger child to deal with, maybe because when they were small they did not get much of a chance to be a baby and sort of get pleasure out of more or less having a second chance with us as a baby, or perhaps because they feel we are so important to them that they want us to stay real close to them.

It is not always mothers who keep us more baby than we should be. Sometimes we do it ourselves. For example, after our baby brother or sister is born, or if we have been very sick or perhaps just moved to a new house. We want to feel loved, and to have some extra attention, in fact to be like babies again, and so that's how we act and behave and talk.

Of course there are other reasons for being slow to talk. You might be one of a family of 'slow talkers' (but you've got to make sure that your parents really know of others in their families who were like you and just don't use this as an excuse). Other reasons might be that there is something wrong with the way your mouth and tongue move or the way your muscles work, or perhaps you are not lucky enough to be clever, or you might even be very disturbed or one of a number of other good reasons. One reason that is often used is that you are 'tongue-tied'. I have heard quite a lot of people say this but I don't think it really is a good reason for being slow to talk. It might add to the reason if your tongue has been snipped, because this is a painful thing to happen to anybody.

Once we can get our tongue and all the other parts we need started on the job of talking we usually go ahead and talk very well. On the other hand we might talk funny. One big way of talking funny is to not talk clearly, to not make the sounds and words come out properly. This is what people call 'baby talk'. We can usually turn baby talk on and off whenever we like. It often depends on who is listening to us, and if we happen to find out that our parents don't like us doing it, we will often use this to make them angry and to get what we want from them.

Sometimes though, talking in this way isn't done on purpose, but seems to have something to do with getting sounds out right. Like when you should say 'dog' you say 'gog', or 'dood' for 'good'. Maybe instead of water you say 'lawter', or 'sish' for 'fish', or 'lit', for 'sit', or all sorts of other things like this. It's this kind of trouble with sounds. Instead of saying 'train' you make it come out like 'too too tain', or when you should say 'apple' you use 'papple', or 'table' you make into 'talebel', and so on. That is, it's a different kind of language you speak because you add a bit more to some words. It is surprising how many parents, but also other people who should know better, say that there is no reason to worry because you will grow out of this kind of talk. It is true that many of us do, but it is also true that it could be made easier for us to do this with some help. As well as that many of us don't grow out of this funny talk and the longer it goes on the harder it is to stop doing it. But the worst thing about it is how you get to feel about it, when other kids laugh at you, grown ups criticise or try to correct you and especially when you find you're talking differently from other kids. It doesn't only hurt at the time, but it also makes you feel not as good as others and sometimes stops you from wanting to do anything because you reckon you are not really able to do it well. So try to get your parents to find out about your funny talk as soon as they start to get worried about it.

The kind of funny talk that worries parents and us the most is called stuttering or stammering. It's pretty hard on parents to have a child who stutters, because your parents, if you do stutter, are likely to be the kind who are particular about lots of things, including talking. Being so particular or perhaps best called by a grown up word, perfectionistic, they get very upset if you don't talk clearly. Lots of you will have only kind of stuttered, when you were toddlers of two or three or four and then it goes away. For others it hasn't. It's kind of sad when we try very hard to get our words out and have to use different tricks to help. Tricks like screwing up our faces, or swallowing, or jumping around, or pointing, or going 'um', 'er' before the words come out. These tricks go along with repeating letters, or parts of words, or sounds. They are a way of trying to get words out and even if they do look funny or, even worse than funny, they look ugly, it really hurts if other people laugh or growl at us. It's all the things that can get tied up with stuttering that really make it hard to get rid of it. I do not think that anyone really knows all the reasons why we stutter, but we do know if it's only just started and if there are obvious things that have happened to us which make us feel sad or unhappy, then our parents can really help, or take us to someone else who can help us, so that the stutter never really gets started.

If we feel very angry and can't get rid of that angry feeling and kind of keep it in or store it up, we often feel bad inside. This inside feeling might not be seen by anybody else, we might not even know where it comes from, but sometimes this bad feeling gets tied up with talking. If you can see that your parents use angry words and get rid of their bad feelings by talking or shouting you might try this yourself. Being much smaller it is sometimes a bit frightening really to let go of all our angry feelings, so we keep some locked in. It's kind of better for us to lock in feelings than to think that if they came out they could in a special magic sort of way hurt other people. Words or sounds are ways of letting out feelings. A start towards locking in these feelings is to lock in or block off sounds or words. Once this is started it's easy to spread this to other feelings and other sounds and words. In some of us this way of keeping feelings inside is a bit like going back to using baby ways, with baby talk.

Talking funny isn't really funny at all, and most of the time we do it for really good reasons. Of course it's a bit hard for our parents to take if we can't get through to them, and they can't get through to us, but just the same it makes us lose out on a big part of being a child, if we can't really talk well. Talking is a big part of our life so if we talk funny a big part of us is upset. Either we are unhappy and need some extra kind of attention from our parents, or extra loving is not working properly, and we need our parents to see this and to ask other people to help us. Believe me, talking funny is no joke.

How to manage your parents when you have skin troubles

Skin covers most of our body and it also covers up many of our troubles. There are sayings about our skin like 'beauty is only skin deep', 'some people have the hide of a rhinoceros'—all ways of showing how our skin can 'talk' about ourselves. You may know that our skin can behave in all kinds of ways. It can change colour, it can sweat, it can swell up. It has hair growing on it, and it can get rid of that hair.

Also it is one part of us through which we can make very close contact with other people and with things. We can touch and be touched through our skins.

Right from the start our skin shows how we feel. When we are babies and cry we often get very red, particularly if we are frustrated, displeased or angry. We get cradle cap, sweat rashes and nappy rash. These are amongst the earliest things that mothers may tend to worry about. The way in which mothers look after their baby's nappy rash may tell you a lot about how they will turn out as mothers. Some mothers spend hours and hours bathing baby, powdering, changing nappies, putting on lots of different creams and ointments. They seem to spend so much time doing these things, because it worries them that their baby is not clean or that the rash (even if very minor) will disturb baby's sleep, or even because they imagine the nappy rash will spread all over their baby. Deep down some of these mothers are worried that they themselves might catch the rash or even worse that they gave it to us. While all this fuss is going on we are being over handled, over stimulated and deprived of sleep and comfort and peaceful routine. It might even be that this kind of over-protective mothering leads to all kinds of difficulties between us and mother later on.

Not all mothers are like that. Some are just right, and some mothers do the exact opposite of over-mothering and neglect our bottom and its covering rash, leave us in wet nappies for hours and never try to heal our skin. They somehow pretend that babies can't really feel very much and ignore us. We soon learn that the discomfort of our bottom, which may make us cry, is very similar to the discomfort of being hungry or the discomfort of colic, none of which get as much attention. It is a bit like a 'barrier' between us and the outside world (and the people in that world), to have a nappy rash or, even worse, sores all over our skin. No one wants to touch us and we get used to being by ourselves without much care or attention, kind of alone and sorry for ourselves at first, and then after a while out of touch with other people.

Washing is often another area of battle between us and our parents. Most of us, especially when we are little, seem to delight in getting dirty. It is part of the making a mess that all toddlers enjoy so much. To us being dirty is just an everyday event, but it's a way of annoying mother. Dirty hands and feet, faces and hair, as well as clothes, need to be washed according to the rules that adults have. After all, they say that dirt breeds germs and that being grimy is a sign of bad breeding. We don't really go for these kinds of explanations, so a battle results, depending on how stern mothers and fathers are and how rigidly they insist on rules of cleanliness; so we learn that we must keep fairly clean or even very clean, often so clean that the slightest bit of dirt or stain of anything has to be washed off immediately. Most of us make a compromise between our parents' need for us to be clean and our wish to be a bit dirty. The best you can hope for is that it's mainly left up to you as to when you get clean or when you stay dirty. This kind of gives you a chance to watch your parents, see what rules they stick to for themselves, and then you can either copy them or change their rules to suit yourselves.

One of the skin troubles that most effectively acts as a barrier is eczema. Eczema seems to run in some families, but others of us are the first to get it. To many people eczema is like a rude word, something meaning dirty or diseased and bad or shameful. It is not surprising that mothers whose children have eczema start to think all kinds of terrible thoughts about the eczema. They might think that they themselves caused it, often because they felt, in part at least, that they did not want to have us. They sometimes might think that it is badness coming out of us, feeling that we are like someone else they know or knew who also was bad, and that somehow we had this badness passed on.

Whatever they feel for you, if you have bad eczema (and luckily most children only have mild eczema) then it's likely that you will be a pretty disturbed child by the time you get rid of your eczema. In part this will be because of the barrier, the trouble your skin and its coating of eczema will make in your ability to make contact with people. Mother's feelings about you and your skin and her handling of you (she might not be able to touch you, hug you or cuddle you freely) will be very important to you. Probably the most important thing will be what treatment you get. Because eczema can seem so difficult to treat and because it sometimes gets very bad, people who have to treat you and your eczema may get very frustrated and angry. There are lots of very cruel things that can be called treatment. Some of these may appear to be necessary, but although they don't harm or hurt the people who apply them they certainly both hurt and harm us. I wonder if our parents can imagine what it must feel like to be tied down in a cot with arms and legs spread eagled, arms unable to move, especially if you are itching all over and really feel you need to scratch; or worse still your arms and legs might be tied into splints with straps that cut into your skin. Sometimes children who have eczema over most of their bodies are covered in bandages so completely that the only parts you can see are the eyes, nostrils and mouth. This bandaging can make it very hard for us to form a picture of our own body.

Unfortunately it is mainly the mothers who have to treat their children who have eczema. There are a lot of angry feelings that you get if you are constantly being bathed, bandaged, having ointment and lotions put on, skin peeled off and being put in splints and special beds, not to mention having pains and itch and getting medicines, tablets, injections, special foods and diets of all types. Because mother is the closest to you and has to carry out most of the treatment, but also because of the way she feels about you, it's most likely that it is mother who you will feel most angry about. Partly because of feeling so angry we often get pretty hard to live with. As we get older we find ways of trying to get rid of our anger—for instance, refusing to take medicine, pulling off splints and bandages, temper tantrums, breaking things and lots more. But worst of all we will also be angry with ourselves—angry that we are the ones who have got eczema and the ones who have got the terrible itch. So when the itch starts we scratch and scratch and scratch, perhaps much more than we really need to. Sometimes we might even scratch the skin away till it bleeds. Parents will not be able to understand how we can do this, how we can hurt ourselves so much, because they would find it hard to know how angry we can get. Eczema is a cruel disease to have, cruel to children and parents, but also to the doctors and others who try to help treat it. Luckily most children get rid of it eventually. It is better when the feelings they have, as well as their skin, are given some help.

There are other ways that our skin might show how we feel. In fact lots of different kinds of spots and rashes, lumps and swellings might be in part connected with your feelings. There is quite a connection between the way you see yourselves on the outside and the way you feel about yourself inside. Some of us have acne, usually when we are teenagers. Although no one really says it to you, you'll probably feel that all the dirt and badness inside you is coming out onto your skin, Not infrequently teenagers who get acne are not very happy people. they have doubts about themselves, are unsure of their roles at home, school and amongst their friends, feel they can't do anything that is worth while or get very ashamed of themselves. To make it worse for us when acne does appear we may be criticised by other people about being dirty and not washing ourselves. This makes us feel even worse because it confirms our thoughts about ourselves. The worst thing out of all this is once you feel bad or, as adults call it, feel 'depressed', you tend to neglect your skin and not to wash as often as you should and so aggravate the acne.

For most of us our skin will not get us into much trouble. We might have a few rashes or cuts or sores. In summer we will get sunburnt or peel. At times we will get measles or chicken pox, but in general our skin will remain a good cover between us and the outside world. However, for all of you there is a possibility that something or somebody will get 'under your skin'. If it happens that your mother or father or perhaps a grandparent or even brother, sister or cousin or aunt are annoying you and making you real mad you might not be able to show them how angry you are because you are too small. Now although you can't see these angry feelings, it's just as if they are stored up inside you, perhaps just 'under your skin' and then you might have a terrible need to scratch. Scratching might get rid of the itches, but it really does not get rid of the feelings you have for someone who has 'got under your skin'.

It's nice to be beautiful, to have nice clear skin. It's hard to keep skin free of trouble if feelings get caught up inside us and can only get out through changes in our skin. Perhaps the hardest part of having skin is that these days most of it is so visible to everyone else, especially on the beach in summer. But just as we can't help having skin, we can't help sometimes having rashes and pimples and bumps and things like that. The biggest problem really is when our parents get side-tracked by the way we look and get involved in treating it or having someone else treat it for us. This has to be done of course and we are glad we can rely on them to help us in this way. But it would be nice to know that our parents could pay attention to how we feel and not just to how we look. After all ugliness like beauty is often just skin deep.

We are people

How to handle your parents when you can't sleep

Going to sleep should be a good feeling—a feeling of peace and quiet. And yet for many of us getting to sleep is not easy. There seem to be several kinds of troubles tied up with sleep. The first is 'going to bed' trouble. Here it seems to largely be a question of time, what time we go to bed. Another problem is 'going to sleep' trouble. That is once we get to bed we can't get to sleep. A third one is the 'staying asleep' kind of trouble. This is usually where nightmares and dreams kind of stop you from sleeping—it's really part of the world of magic we live in at night time.

Sleeping is such a common thing to do it's a wonder we have any kind of trouble with it, but we do. These troubles seem in some ways tied up with the patterns of sleep we develop from just after we are born. As babies we mostly spend a lot of our time sleeping. Somehow it seems to fill in the time till we are old enough to stay awake. Before long we get to be old enough to stay awake for part of the day. By the time we are able to walk a bit we think we are old enough to stay awake all day. Parents seem to have different ideas about this, because according to their rules we need to sleep at midday or in the afternoon, or some time just when everything that is at all interesting seems to be going on. As soon as we get this misunderstanding sorted out and get our views on the matter accepted, by getting old enough to stay awake all day, we are in for another battle. Now it is the business of what time do we go to bed at night.

This time business seems very important to our parents. Mostly we can't see what all the fuss is about. Sometimes parents expect us to have a concept of time before we even know how to count, and often before we can think about time in the complicated way adults do. Parents have different ideas about what is the right time for bed. Some of them expect us to be in bed at exactly the same time each night. Now this is a pretty hard thing to do. Other parents don't seem to care what time they go to bed, and don't tell their children to go to bed, so the children just go at any old time. But most parents don't insist on an exact time each day, unless it suits them to and then they stick to that time like glue. Usually it only suits them to do this if they want to go out, have visitors or want to go to bed themselves. One way or another we spend most of our evenings involved in some kind of argument about when we should go to bed, and, once we are in bed, when we should go to sleep.

Although you would think going to bed is an easy matter, it really is very complicated. For most of us going to bed might mean one of a number of different things. For instance, we might feel going to bed is like going away or even like being sent away (this especially after a few years of being told to go to bed or to our bedroom when we are being punished). Going to bed could be like being separated from and losing someone we love, particularly mother. For some of us bedtime is a bit like being tied down or restrained or stopped from doing what we want to do. It might even feel as if we are dying. For most children, and especially when we are small, lying still and not moving is a bit like being dead. But probably the main feeling we have about going to bed is that it is a way of missing out on something, whether it's getting attention, seeing T.V., watching mother bake a cake, parents fighting, or most commonly missing out on staying up as long as our older brothers and sisters do. So if we have even one of these reasons for not going to bed, we reckon our reason is a pretty good one and we probably get involved in an argument over bedtime.

It's pretty hard to tell even mum or dad that you don't want to go to bed because you are frightened you'd die. It might even be so frightening that you can't talk at all, but just cry. Now most parents will put up with this for a little time, but if they can't get through to you and you can't get through to them, then there is sure to be trouble. You've probably relied on their being kind and controlled and helping you overcome your fears, but they don't realise that by losing control of themselves, they only make the whole thing harder for you. You can no longer rely on them. Here we get all tied up in what's called, by adults, a 'vicious circle'. You're frightened, your parents lose control, this frightens you more, they get even more rattled, you scream louder, they shout more and so on till bedtime is a complete shambles.

On the other hand you might not be frightened of bed, you might know very well that going to bed is perfectly safe, but you might also know that your not going to bed is a way of annoying your parents. You might feel that there is something you have missed out on, or there is some need to get your own back. If you've learned over the years that you can annoy your parents by somehow getting them out of their routine, then bedtime is a pretty good opportunity to test out your observation. You just have to try any number of delaying tactics, like asking for another drink, having to go to the toilet, giving mother a special goodnight kiss, needing to talk to father about something that is so important that it can't wait till tomorrow, and so on. Better still, wait until you have been put to bed, tucked in, had the light put out and then up you get and go into the lounge. Usually this is just in time to hear mother saying to dad, 'Thank God he is in bed,' or 'I'll murder him if he gets up tonight,' or some other words that you are really waiting to hear, because then you know for sure that your tactics have worked. Even more annoying for parents are the ways you have of insisting on having the door open to exactly the right amount, or blankets tucked in to a precise degree of tightness, or the windows open to a certain extent. If you really quibble over these, especially if you don't get your way and start to scream and carry on, then you're sure to get your parents really annoyed, because you've won the going to bed fight, at least for that night.

These going to bed fights are largely between real people, that is, you and your parents. The fights are out in the open, the battle field is about three to six feet in size and you've got a pretty good chance of winning. It is different when 'going to sleep' troubles start. This kind of trouble might just be an extension of the pitched battle over going to bed. Again it might be a fight between real people with some new tricks thrown in. On the other hand it might change a bit into a fight with make believe people. Just as you close your eyes or even before you do, a ghost may come out of your cupboard and slowly twist and twirl till it is sitting on the end of your bed. Sometimes a green-eyed monster with no hands or feet but with great big shining teeth might slowly creep through the key-hole. Little elves or goblins with flashing lights for eyes and bags full of human bones on their backs could creep out of the space by your chest of drawers. An undertaker with a black top hat and with a green face may suddenly appear at the foot of your bed, witches with buck teeth, straggly hair and long dirty fingernails could glide in the window. You might not be sure if you are awake or already asleep, but for sure you will scream and cry for help. When your parents come running in to you you might be able to describe what you saw, but they will probably tell you to stop being so silly and go to sleep, or they will reason with you and explain very logically (for an adult) that there are no such things as ghosts or witches, monsters and boogey men. Somehow their explanations can't quite make the memory of what you saw go away. You might doubt whether mother and father really know about these things, because after all you reckon the monsters are coming to get you and not them. Even when you get a bit older the monsters and ghosts might stay there. It's possible that they have been with you so long that they get to be part of your way of life, they might even become a sort of friend to whom you can talk and tell your troubles. However, usually they don't become friends, they stay enemies, only by now you've learnt ways of getting rid of them, or perhaps means of making sure they can't attack you. To you it's perfectly sensible to lock your window and draw the curtains closed to an exact spot each night, to sweep under your bed and in all the corners each evening, to clean out and reorganise your cupboard daily or to put locks on your door and even chains and things like 'time bombs' around your bed. It's sensible to you because you believe in magical ways of protecting yourselves. Unfortunately it is not sensible to your parents because they have kind of lost their sense of magic. They have not really lost it altogether—just enough to make them very annoyed when you use magic; probably because they wish lots of times that they could also use magic, and get annoyed that it does not work with them.

Just as we get used to going to bed and then going to sleep a third kind of problem might come up. This is called nightmares or night terrors or just plain bad dreams. All of you will have had some dreams; probably even before you were old enough to talk properly, dreams have started. It's just that you can't tell mother about them because you do not have the words to describe 'pictures' you see. Once it was said there were only two kinds of dreams, good and bad. Now we know that there are lots of kinds, but we know that a part of each of our dreams is made up of a bit of 'real life' and another part might be made up of a kind of wish or it might come from a fear. All the parts get tied together by a magical way of thinking, so they seem to be different or strange to us, or even weird. If they are particularly frightening, especially if somehow it seems as if we are going to be hurt or that we might lose a fight or fall over a cliff or have a car accident, then we wake up. This waking up is a kind of escape from the dream, running back to the safety of being awake and with people we know and trust. So as we dream or just as we wake from the dream we usually call out for our parents. Nearly all parents will come very quickly if they hear their child crying in the night, especially if it sounds like a frightened cry. Somehow I think that parents kind of remember how frightening their own dreams are or have been and can feel straight away that their children need help. Now this is one of the times that shows which parents can cope with their children and which can't. Those parents that just pacify you and reassure you that they are there, able to help you and don't panic or growl at you are doing well. Unfortunately some parents get very upset if their children have bad dreams. They may take their children back to their bed, growl at them or even at times beat their children to make them 'come to their senses'. What they are really doing is telling you that they are just as frightened as you are and that does not really help you at all. Sometimes we make use of our parents not being able to cope, and seem to have nightmares every night, or at least very often. Not uncommonly it is at almost the same time at night. Probably you have found out that it's the quickest way to get into mum's bed or that it's easier to sleep with mum or dad in fact than just in your dreams, or even that it feels safer to be awake with mum or dad in your room.

Most times you wake at night it will be because of dreams, but sometimes there are other good reasons for not staying asleep. It might be at night time that your parents argue or even more often it's night time when strange noises come from your parent's bedroom, a room which you might feel has secrets which you might like to know about. So you might stay awake or awaken especially to listen to parents argue or to try to understand these secret sounds. Just as our parents have secrets, so do we, and night time is the chosen time for secrets. I know that teenagers often like to wake up to 'think' or if they have someone close to their own age to 'talk to'. Both are secret kinds of things to do, especially at night. Others might use the night to get out of bed, to wander around the house asleep (called sleepwalking), pretending to be asleep (also called sleepwalking), or stealthily and on purpose. This often is to discover secrets, but sometimes it's a revolt, a way of fighting a battle with our parents to do something that is forbidden. Sometimes we carry our wishes further and steal out of bed, out of the window or door and act out our wishes under the cloak of darkness.

We really have wishes about what we would like our parents to do when we have these sleep troubles. We wish they would be just as certain to ask us why we don't want to go to bed as they are about the exact time they determine we must keep to. Once we get caught up in our battle, it would be best for us if they won, and pretty quickly. If they insist we go and we can see they really mean it, are not going to change their minds or feel guilty about being firm with us, then we reckon we may as well let them win. Once we are in bed and try our getting out again stunt, it's much easier if our parents kind of ignore us. This really shows us that there is nothing they are worried about, that's the best kind of reassurance we can get. We all do need reassurance if we have nightmares, but we can do without getting into parents' beds, being growled at or even belted. We can maybe then wish them goodnight and be sure not to see them again at least till morning comes.

You can see that sleep, especially those parts of sleep like going to bed, going to sleep and staying asleep, can be full of troubles, full of fights usually between you and your parents. When we are little we often say things like, 'Sleep is all right if you wake up again,' or 'Sleep frightens me,' or 'If I go to sleep I fight with my mummy, she's bigger, so I had better stay awake.' If you feel like that you had better put your head under your pillow, pull up your blankets, sleep tight and hope you don't fight in your sleep tonight. If you *really* can't sleep ask your parents for a sleeping pill. That's what they mostly do.

How to explain to your parents when you have frights and fears

There are all sorts of fears that children and adults have. Sometimes it's pretty obvious what we are frightened of and no-one is too mystified about this. Lots of our parents are frightened by things that are happening around them in the world like wars and bombs, and by what will happen to them when they are old and are dying. These sorts of fears are more or less normal. In just the same way lots of us have more or less normal fears that come as we are growing up, and often go by the time we are no longer children.

Often though the sorts of fears that we have don't seem very real. They don't seem to be the sorts of things that should frighten us, and often this is a great puzzle to our parents and also, of course, to ourselves. This is because our fears get hidden behind a kind of camouflage. The camouflage often changes but the fears stay the same. When we get frightened of the dark, of dogs or of monsters and machines, it's usually because we think these kinds of things threaten to hurt us. We feel that they will pounce out on us. Especially in the dark, we don't know if they are really there, but we behave as if they are. It's because they might be there and it's hard to be convinced that they are not.

Our parents usually say, 'There is nothing to be frightened of, it's just that you can't see in the dark,' 'Dogs won't hurt you, except of course some dogs which are fierce and you've got to be careful of them.' This is sometimes a bit confusing for us because we don't know which ones to be afraid of and which ones are all right. There aren't really any monsters but there are monster machines, and our parents talk about them and so do books and newspapers and television.

It all seems to start when we are babies. We all learn to be afraid of being hurt, which is the thing that is really behind all our frights and fears. If we get hurt once we don't want it ever to happen again. Sometimes we hurt others and then we wonder about what it is in us that makes us able to hurt other people, even sometimes those who we love. We don't want to hurt people we love, and we don't want to be hurt by them, but we do and we are.

It's something that we have to get used to and most of us do, more or less. Those of us who don't manage it soon come to be afraid not only of some people hurting us, but of all people, people in crowds and people on their own, animals, the wind and thunder and lightning, noise and light and machines. That's being very afraid, so afraid that at times we might not even be able to go out or do anything in case we get hurt.

Sometimes not being able to separate from mother starts in a real kind of fear.[1] This fear is of being separate, particularly being separated from mother. When we are babies we feel we are joined to everything around us, to our bed and to the blankets, to mother and mother's feelings, to our bath and the water in it. As we get older, we have to separate, but to some of us this is terribly hard. We have to because we are growing up and we need to be independent. But even this can be very frightening. Sometimes you can see babies who scream and scream if they are away from mother. They are obviously terrified and feel terrible. You can see little children cringe and try to make themselves seem very small, so as not to be noticed if they are away from mother. To be away from her feels as if anything could happen to us—we could starve or we could get lost, but especially we feel we might lose mother. It's not that we feel we have lost her, only that we might. Here as well as in other places, we sometimes sort of camouflage this kind of fear behind a wall of thumb sucking, rocking and all sorts of other interesting habits.[2]

Sometimes our fears are hidden by tantrums,[3] and other times it's by not being able to go to sleep or waking up at night when we have

---

[1] See *How to handle your parents when you won't go to school.*

[2] See *How to manage your parents when you are sucking your thumb* and *How to educate your parents about rocking and rolling.*

what is called a nightmare or a night terror. These may be just ordinary everyday fears but sometimes are so bad and so horrible that we can't bear to think about them when we are awake. When we are asleep they seem to creep out from inside us and although they are camouflaged in all sorts of weird and wonderful ways the feeling of being afraid is there in all of them.[4]

One thing of course that will often make us fearful is our parents. These are usually angry parents, parents that show us all the time exactly how much hate they have inside them. Sometimes they show it to us and they treat us as if they hate us, and sometimes they show it only to other people, but this is almost as frightening. It's awful for us to see, that they, on whom we rely so much, and who seem to have so much power and so much say about what happens to us, have all this hate in them. It makes us frightened of the same kinds of feelings in ourselves and often we are not sure whether to show how we feel or try to hide it. This business of hiding your feelings when they are angry ones is something that you can't get away with for long. Even when we manage it while we are little, as we grow up we start to get all sorts of different illnesses that seem to go along with being unable to express how we feel, things like asthma and ulcers and high blood pressure.

Our parents can make us frightened in other ways too. Sometimes this is because they themselves always seem to be so terribly frightened of everything. They may be frightened of spaces or of being alone or of heights or of people or of loud noises. Sometimes our mothers are frightened of men and sometimes our fathers are frightened of women. We watch them and we see what they do and we feel what they feel and pretty soon we are like they are. Sometimes we will get so frightened and so anxious that we have to do all sorts of funny and peculiar things to make ourselves feel better and these are often called rituals.[5]

There are lots of fears of course that are the sorts of things that we should expect to feel when we are little. Some of them are real but they get mixed up with unreal things. Real tigers and giant sabertooth tigers. Real alsations and fierce man-eating dogs; real rockets and flying saucers. Fears of being too small and of being too tall. Fears of being too fat and too thin. Of having periods and not having periods. Fears of

[3] See *How to handle your parents when you are having a temper tantrum.*
[4] See *How to handle your parents when you can't sleep.*
[5] See *How to educate your parents when you have started being too clean.*

getting to be an adult and fears of staying a child. It's not being able to connect things with reality that is often the basis of many of our fears.

You would think that our parents would be the first ones to understand the sorts of things that are going through our minds over all of this, but unfortunately they are often the last ones. They seem to get embarrassed or even anxious over the fact that we are frightened and they don't like other people to know what's going on. Sometimes they will get so angry with us for being frightened they will beat us and think that in some way this will make us brave. Sometimes they laugh at us, which they call trying to kid us out of it, but this is even worse. Lots of times we know that we have no real reason to be frightened but no matter how ridiculous we seem what we really want is their sympathy and support, logic, explanation and understanding. Most of us who have parents who can be like that when we need them will gradually come to understand things that have really frightened us, and one day be able to laugh at them ourselves.

Lastly I think the people we should really be sorry for are the adults and children who are never afraid of anything, because being afraid is always, in a way, being afraid of losing something. People who are never afraid don't seem to have anything to lose.

How to handle your parents when they discover you have been masturbating

This can be a real problem. Almost any parent seems to get upset if they find their son or daughter masturbating. It is bad enough if they catch you doing it in bed or in your room but if somebody else points it out to them, like your teacher or a kind lady next door or your grandparents, then your parents seem to get very distressed and often angry. The way for them to get most angry over this is for you to do it out in the open, right in front of them. Many of them of course don't have a very liberal attitude towards this sort of thing at all. Some of them even have ideas which are much more frightening than masturbation is.

Sometimes they call masturbation 'self abuse' which seems to mean that you are doing yourself some sort of harm. Even quite intelligent parents sometimes believe that you'll either become a moron, a pervert, a degenerate, a madman or very weak from doing it. Of course if they really believe this, you have to sympathise with them a little bit because no-one would want to think that their son or daughter was going to turn out that way. As a matter of fact a lot of doctors used to believe that sort of thing not too long ago. Fortunately nowadays most of them understand about it and if mum or dad is not too embarrassed to ask, the doctor will usually reassure them.

It is very hard to stop doing something that gives you pleasure, especially when you are a child. Adults forget this because they often have to get so used to doing without pleasant things that they learn to kind of control when and how they get pleasure. They can almost turn it on and off like a tap. It is even harder to stop masturbating if as well as pleasure you get other kinds of feelings out of doing it. For instance, some of you will learn that masturbating annoys your parents so much, you go on doing it just to get your own back. Or you might like the added attention you get from your parents because of what you are doing. Very occasionally parents might even encourage you to masturbate, usually because they themselves get a funny kind of pleasure out of watching you do this.

Most people say boys do this more often than girls, but this isn't really so. All sorts of different things are blamed for it too. Some people say if you wear tight clothes it happens and some people say it will start if you've got a slightly disturbed nanny who tries to put you to sleep by stroking your penis or clitoris. I think girls probably do it just as much as boys, but they have the advantage that they can get away with it much more easily. Some of you probably started playing with or touching your penis or clitoris when you were very small. Even in your first few years. Sometimes it isn't so much touching with your hands as rubbing your legs together or other kinds of things like this. It is very difficult for parents to think that their 'baby' is doing this horrible thing. So they usually try to forget it, deny to themselves that it is happening or very occasionally ask a doctor about what this means and what they should do. What is really frightening is the sorts of things that some parents say to their sons when they find out. Some say 'I'll chop it off' or 'A bird will come and bite it off.' Others often say, 'If you keep doing that I will take it away and give it to your little sister,' which is a far more horrifying situation to contemplate. If there is one thing that a boy of about five or six can't stand it's the thought that his penis might be taken away from him, and to think that his sister, who doesn't seem to have one, might get his, is just adding insult to injury. Parents often don't realise the sorts of problems boys have over this and if they overdo this kind of talk there is a good chance that he'll get pretty inhibited over what he can do with his penis, and in fact when he grows up he might never do anything with it where a woman is concerned. Sometimes this not knowing what to do with your penis spreads to not knowing what to do in other ways, so it's important to learn what use your penis is.

The thing most parents don't seem to realise is why we sometimes masturbate. As in a lot of other things, they keep thinking we are just little adults and wonder why we should do this when there are so many other ways that we have of enjoying ourselves. Of course this is partly true, particularly when we get to be a bit older, say twelve or thirteen, but even here we've got difficulties and problems and one of the most important is how we are trying to adjust to some of the fairly adult sexual feelings we have before anybody will really give us the opportunity to fulfil them in any way. When we're younger of course this is even worse. Parents don't seem to want to know that young children can have sort of sexual feelings and they pretend that they never had any themselves. Any child with any kind of sex urge, they think, is some sort of degenerate monster. But we do it in the first place, of course, because it's a rather nice way to feel good. If you are anxious, worried or distressed over something, you find out pretty soon that by doing this you can feel safe and relaxed and warm. Somehow we feel more secure and whatever it is that is bothering us doesn't seem quite so important. In a way it is very much like sucking your thumb or the pleasure of emptying your bowels when you were younger. Of course a lot of parents get pretty nasty about those habits too if they catch you doing them. If you masturbate a lot and don't seem to be able to help doing it whether people are watching you or not, parents don't realise it is because something is making you very anxious or very frightened indeed. They usually react by punishing you dreadfully and sometimes by tying your hands, and other things that are only likely to make you feel worse.

The problem that we have to face is that masturbation is bound up with the whole sex problem, and you know that is something that parents just don't want to face up to. If mother's catch their children masturbating they usually get a terrible shock and then get frightfully embarrassed. It is very difficult to know what to do in a situation like this because you can't really say, 'Sorry, mum and dad, let's forget about it,' because somehow you know that things between you will never be the same again. They won't let it. Mothers often ask dad to talk to you about it. He is usually so embarrassed that he doesn't say anything but belts you instead.

If dad does come in and belt you, well this of course only adds to the problem that you are already probably having with him, especially if you are around five or six. This is the time as you know when boys more or less 'fall in love' with their mothers. They want to be near them and touch them and kiss them and cuddle them. A lot of mothers like this, but a lot of them can't stand it and get terribly upset and disturbed. The dads of course often laugh it off and that's good enough because you then feel safe and you don't worry about the way you feel. But sometimes dad gets a bit angry and threatening and then all of this business about 'I'll chop it off and give it to your sister' comes up again. This is a very difficult time and if dad overdoes it, the way you feel about him might not be quite the same ever again. Although little girls go through the same sort of phase it looks to be different to boys. They compete with mum in the same way boys compete with dad, but it takes a pretty brave or pretty unhappy girl to really set herself up in competition with the one person who has meant the most to her and who she really loves more than anybody else—mother. Of course sometimes little girls don't have much choice in this and their mothers really set them up so that they can't help but get into difficulties around this time.

It's just as well for parents that most children stop masturbating after a little while, usually as soon as they grow a bit more and find other ways of feeling good and safe and secure. Of course it can be embarrassing and distressing for a parent to see their little boy or girl doing things that other parents call 'dirty'. But it shouldn't be. Not if they understand that it's a way of feeling good and that it shows a need to feel good. The more we do it, and the less control we have over it, the greater is our need and their responsibility in helping us, or if they can't, in finding someone who can. Probably if you can persuade your parents not to take any notice of your masturbating and particularly if they learn not to threaten or punish you for it, then you won't feel too bad about it (the kind of bad that grown ups call guilty). However, if you do, you can be sure that you will be in for all sorts of sexual difficulties when you get to be adult—and then heaven help your children if you catch them masturbating.

How to introduce your parents to playing mummies and daddies

'Let's play mothers and fathers; you be the father and I'll be the mother,' 'Let's play house,' 'If you be the baby I'll be mother and he can be father,' or sayings just like them are what we all have said at some time or other. Usually our parents let us play these kinds of games without getting upset. Some parents don't like this way of playing, some even reckon it's not playing, but real serious and stop us from doing it. Most of us play mothers and fathers just because it's good fun to pretend to be like them. We reckon they seem to have a lot of fun being parents and grown ups, so if we copy them maybe it will be good fun for us too. Somehow it's also a way of showing how curious we are. By playing fathers and mothers we kind of pretend we really know what it's like to be them. In fact it's because we are not sure, are curious enough to want to know and can experiment with different games and ways of pretending, that we get to be more and more like our parents.

Through all this pretending we are really not only playing, but also learning to be like our parents. We learn to act like them and to behave like them. We try out their ideas and make them our own. We might even get to know of their pretendings or imaginations and use those too, for our own. Also it's the feelings and ideas that our parents have, but don't even know about themselves, that we get to learn about and kind of use for ourselves. We get used to the way our parents show their angry feelings, their loving and their sexual feelings, then we copy them and learn how and when and sometimes even why they use these feelings. It's all called a thing by the name of identification'[1].

We assume that our parents know the meaning of all these big words, but usually we are wrong. We are also wrong if we think that our parents know just what goes on in playing mothers and fathers. They really should know because they played pretty much the same games when they were children. They might remember bits of their games, but usually they have forgotten all about them. They don't get a very good chance to learn all our secrets in our mother and father games, because we don't let them. If they start to get interested and get

[1] See *How to handle your parents when you are establishing your identity.*

to creep up close to watch and listen, or if they ask us what we are doing, it's usually best to say 'Just playing' or 'Nothing much,' or even all of a sudden to get real interested way off over there. This is because we know that they are grown up, and adults don't know about children or at least they act as if they don't know. So if they don't know why should we teach them? Also, if they act a bit funny or even are shocked about our games we wonder why they should see it like that. Usually we can't work it out, but we learn that there seems to be something funny or shocking about these games and so we get a bit shy and secretive about doing what our parents think is somehow not right. I suppose that it is really a bit confusing for the parents, because most games of mothers and fathers can get pretty complicated.

There are all kinds of ways of playing these games. There is the straight out mother and father game; if you're mother and I'm father and then we just do what mothers and fathers do. Then there is the game where there are two mothers and maybe two fathers and this gets a bit hard to follow unless you happen to know about wishing for different kinds of parents. Also, there are babies and older children that get to be part of the game and even aunts and grandmothers, grocers, butchers and policemen, but not teachers. No, you never get teachers in the game of mothers and fathers. The teacher game is a different one altogether. We know a lot of our parents and teachers don't know that parents can't be teachers and teachers can't be parents, at least not our teachers and our parents. Having sorted out the different people is about as far as parents get, because after that it gets to be even more mixed up. What with different kinds of talking, different ways of crying, all sorts of things that get done, places that get visited and so on, it's pretty hard when adults only have adult rules to work things out by. We have a different lot of rules, or to our parents it perhaps seems we have no rules at all. But even with all this it's pretty strange that our parents don't seem to know about playing mothers and fathers, because it's really just being like them, or at least pretending to be like them. Perhaps adults don't recognise themselves very easily.

If they look very closely they may find out that most of these mother and father games are exact bits of real life, family life. The family's way of behaving is right out in the open for every one to see, but often it's not the bits of their lives that they want anyone else to see. Because they don't want anyone to know about these things they pretend so hard to themselves that no-one does know it. They don't recognise it when it's right in front of them.

Adults seem to try almost as hard to believe that children don't know much. (That is probably true only half the time, because the other half they expect children to know everything.) We really are much better at knowing what adults think and feel and pretend than they give us credit for. We get to be aware of lots of things. If our parents knew what we know, they might be very angry, or blush, or get ashamed, or things like that. For instance, most of our parents who talk real loudly because they are trying to act big would be really surprised to learn that their children know that they want to act big. In just the same way and with the same reason (except it's more logical in us) we talk real loudly. We get to know that our parents fight with each other and that they call each other secret names. Sometimes good and sometimes bad names, but often they sound both good and bad at the same time. We find out that they are shy about being naked, or about kissing, or about cuddling each other, so when we play mothers and fathers we act real coy and shy about those things too. Sometimes we get to learn that our fathers (and less often our mothers) really love money and are kind of misers about it, or that the only thing that they really care about is being better than anybody else. Maybe they would rather drink beer, play cards or back race horses than play with us. All these kinds of secrets get put into our games; often they change in the way they come out. The secrets might look only little, or they might get blown up real big, but always they are in some ways true to life.

One of the main truths about life is that each of us has the same kind of way of sorting out the connections between the three most important people in our life—ourself, mother and father. When we find out that there are people in the world we all first kind of connect ourselves with mother. It does not make any difference if we are boys or girls. We then get to know, and get connected with, father. Some families stay just like that, with only three in them. Some get a few more, some get lots more. No matter how many people there are, the three of most importance to each of us are always the same. After a while it's a bit different for boys and for girls. Boys try even harder to be just like their fathers and girls like their mothers (identification again). Trying to be like someone else means having the same things and doing the same as that someone. We try to be the same size, do the same work, wear the same clothes, talk the same way and own the same kind of things. If it can't be exactly the same we try to get as near to it as possible. One thing that parents reckon they own is each other, so fathers kind of own mothers and mothers own fathers. Because we try to be just the same as father or as mother we try to own mother or father. Now this can lead to problems—the main one is that mother already belongs to father, or the other way round. So to take over we have to steal, or in some kind of crooked way win the one we want. We have to get rid of our rival, the parent who is the same sex as we are. Then we could have mother or father to ourselves. It's bad luck that lots of other reasons seem to get in the way of our getting what we want. In the first place we are small, much smaller and much less strong than mother and father. Although we have heard of a little guy called 'David' taking on a giant like 'Goliath' that somehow does not make it any easier if we get down to the job. Another trouble is that we identify with both our parents, so as well as wanting to get rid of father or mother, we love them and want to keep them both.

In the long run it's just as well that these kind of problems happen inside us, in the part of us that thinks, feels and pretends. So we don't really have to fight, or steal, or lose someone who is important to us. But even though it's not for real it's still kind of hard for us. Because it's so hard, boys usually give up, so do girls. We have to make do with second best. We just keep all these troubles in our world of make-believe. Playing games and especially playing mothers and fathers is a big part of our world of make believe so we put into these games a lot of our ideas and feelings about our three most important people. Some of our feelings and ideas get pretty close to what grown ups call 'sexy'. This to them usually means just one thing, but to us it's lots of different ways of thinking and feeling. Right from the time we are only months old we find a kind of good feeling coming from different parts of our body. First of all it's probably our mouths; sucking, eating, chewing and so on give us our food and fill our stomachs, but from our mouths and lips we also get other feelings. Sometimes these make us feel really peaceful. Being able to suck on a cigarette, chew gum or slurp beer seems to make adults feel the same. For a few of us chewing peanuts or crunching candy or even bits of glass gets to be a bit exciting. We all like having kissing games with, and giving real slurpy kisses to, our parents. After a while we kind of learn it is fun doing it with other people. We see grown ups going around kissing lots of other people, so that's one reason we like to kiss other kids.

Another way of getting excited when we are small is to kind of get thrown around by our dads or bounced up and down. These sudden movements make for a bit of a scare, but after a while it's a thrill as well. We get to be able to do this for ourselves and to play games when we roll around, hop, jump, twist and twirl. After a bit longer it gets to be kind of fun to do this with someone else. Boys play wrestling and so do girls. When we get to be about four to five it's part of father and mother games to get fun out of bouncing about together or curling up under blankets or rugs or in cubby houses and inside tents. Mothers and fathers all seem to like doing these things in their beds, so if we are going to copy them we've got to do it in our pretend beds. Sometimes we even get to be able to do it in our real beds if we can be secret enough about it and so quiet that our parents don't know we've sneaked into our rooms. When we find ourselves in bed with someone else it's easy to touch or get touched on our bottom parts. Now this can get to be real good. Even when we are little, just babies, we touch our bottom parts. This is a bit easier for boys, because they stick out more than girls and that thing sticking out kind of often gets in the way. A boy's penis gets caught up in his nappy and between his legs. When he is in the bath or at other times when his pants are off he can hang on to it with his hands. Girls really don't have as much to hang onto, but rubbing and stroking can make just as good feelings start in their bottoms. After a while these good kind of feelings get to be used when we feel we need them. Later on we can even get to use these feelings as parts of games with other children. We let the others know about our feelings and we are not really surprised that others feel just like we do. This to grown ups seems strange, because adults often say that they can't understand their own sexy feelings and especially that they are sure that no one else could feel like they do themselves. Maybe it's harder to be real sexy when you get to be an adult. Anyway, we get to be pretty proud of our bottom parts because it's one part of ourselves that everyone shows some interest in and most people show a real lot of interest in. So we take it for granted that it's the thing to do to show everyone what our bottom parts look like.

This business of showing ourselves to other children and also to grown ups seems a good way of 'showing off'. Even if we are pretty proud of our bottom parts we kind of wonder what others look like and if others reckon their own bottoms are any better than ours. We all do this, but some do it more than they are supposed to. There seem to be several kinds of children that show off their bottoms a real lot. It might be the thing at home to walk around without clothes, to have baths and showers, to sit on the toilet and leave all the doors open. Maybe even to do most things like eating meals, sweeping up and doing the washing while being naked. To us there does not seem to be any reason why this should not go on all the time. But we know that even though grown ups pretend by doing these things they are what they call 'broad minded', they really have a thing about their own bottoms and need to prove something to themselves or to other people. So we kind of copy them, only they don't know we are really copying them. On the other hand our parents might have an even more obvious thing about their bottoms and hide themselves all the time. It gets to be like it's all a great big secret. Because we can't understand this, we go the other way and let our secrets out of the bag (or rather, out of our pants). It's a funny thing, but some of these parents who hide themselves so much secretly want to show themselves off, but they can't. So they try to encourage us to do it for them. That kind of thing is pretty sick. Parents don't usually think that they are sick, they often reckon that we are sick and sometimes they really believe we are.

But it's not sick to do any of these things. To us it's normal. It's really us just getting to be grown up. But the disturbing thing is it's not quite grown up. To make it worse some adults are not quite grown up either. So adults say that it's wrong for us to like looking at bottom parts. But this looking business is pretty common in adults. They look at pictures of big girls with no clothes on, or girls with bare middle or top. They put half naked girls beside motor cars, refrigerators, electric blankets, coffee jars and lots of other things that somehow don't seem to have anything to do with sex. Then they call this advertising. They go to the beach and watch girls in bikinis, or to the wrestling to watch men in shorts, or to the ballet and watch both men and girls in pretty tight clothes. There are all kinds of excuses that grown ups give themselves and others to explain why they look. They get kind of angry if you catch them doing it and ask what they are looking at. If they catch us looking they get angry with us and somehow this makes them feel a bit better about their own looking. Still, I suppose, they are all just like we are, looking for the good feelings it gives them. If our parents could understand that, then they would understand why we need to play mummies and daddies too.

How to get your parents to tell you about the birds and the bees

All those stories about the 'birds and the bees' are really stories about babies. It might be hard for some people to believe, but if you really think hard about it you can see some sorts of connections. For examples birds, bees and babies all start with the letter 'b', or again bird, bees and baby all have four letters, or yet again they are all animal. Even though we can see these sorts of connections it's pretty hard to know that their common association, anyway according to adults, is reproduction. Lots of parents tell their children how they came to be alive just like the birds and the bees or even sometimes that the birds and the bees brought us into our home, all of which is pretty irrational. It's really very strange to think that this business of babies and reproduction and pregnancy and birth, which is after all a pretty factual and basic business, seems to get hidden behind all of these funny stories about other animals.

It gets hidden there by adults. And yet even though they seem to have to hide this real piece of life, they never really get to discovering that we also hide our ideas about babies and birth. Of course we think a great deal about these topics, and even play games about it.[1] We play about it a lot, but we don't talk about it. If our parents encouraged us to, well, tell them a few things, that would probably make them blush, but I don't see that ever happening, anyway not unless they read this chapter.

The further you go into this business the more silly it seems to become, because not only birds and bees are involved, but also storks, and cabbages and strawberry patches, and black bags and seeds and God and 'being close to mummy's heart' and being 'carried in a special place'. These all seem to have a bit of something secret tied up with them, something mysterious but, when you really look, it's something false; false and not factual. It's a bit hard to get across to our parents that what we need to know is fact, and what makes us go along with all this falsehood is our lack of facts. These stories mainly come from our parents. It comes from the fact that our parents have once been children and then they too thought about these matters just as much as we do, and they didn't have enough facts to go on, so they asked their parents. Later they got so confused about it all, they tried very hard to forget

[1] See *How to introduce your parents to playing mummies and daddies.*

the whole thing. Only when they again have to think about it because we ask them to, they bring us the ideas they got as children—birds and bees and storks and cabbages and seeds and God and so on. They do fit very nicely into children's ideas. They must, otherwise parents wouldn't have been allowed to get away with using these ideas for so long.

The way that we think about these things, and the way that our parents once thought about them, often starts with eating. We children eat. If we eat we get fat tummies; so does mother when she is having a baby—conclusion: babies come from eating. They come from eating food, maybe they come from drinking milk, that's kind of connected for all of us with being a baby. Maybe it isn't only food that gets to be inside us, it's also seeds, that's what we get told when we ask—we grow from seeds. How do they get inside? They get there by eating of course. Where do these seeds come from—from father. So it's what father gives mother that makes children. How does he do it? Father comes home with money which he gives to mummy. Maybe she swallows the money. Father also brings home a cold and gives it to us; maybe he gives germs to mother and we grow from them. All of these things can go into our mouths and our noses, just the same as they can with mother. Maybe if father gives us seeds or food or germs we will get pregnant too. Therefore, we say to ourselves—don't let father too close, we might get pregnant, don't let him feed us or breathe on us.

It is not only by opening our mouths that things get inside us. We have ears and noses and also we have bottoms. We've got pores in our skin. Eyes take things in and any of these openings are suitable for the entry of seeds and germs. But also, things come out of these openings, particularly out of our bottoms—poos and wees. Maybe if they don't come out, if they stay inside they will grow and grow until we are full and fat, full and fat just like mother. So maybe babies come from poos and wees, but that's dirty, it's pooey, it's urkey and so are babies. It's bad to be dirty and pooey, and so it's wrong to think about babies and how they get there.

So maybe we can think of how they get born. This is even more secret.[2] We know baby is being carried inside mother. She's told us. We were put there by God, close to her heart or carried in a special place, but how did we get out. Mother vomits during her pregnancy. She

[2] See *How to bring up your parents when the new baby arrives.*

is carrying a baby inside her, maybe it comes out the same way it gets in, by the mouth—how messy, how bad. Babies aren't all that messy and bad; could they come out with the poos and wees? That's it. Mummy pushes them out through her bottom, she said so, baby comes out of the bottom, that's close to it. Let's leave it like that. But mummy said a special place in her bottom, not where the poos comes from. She must be kidding. Maybe it's somewhere else. Could it be our navel? That's got something to do with babies. Maybe it opens up. Could be the doctor does it with his knife. Mother did say that doctor will help her in hospital. Could be. But that would hurt mother. Let's forget about that. Mother said doctor's black bag brings babies. That's a good idea. Cabbages and strawberry patches are supposed to grow babies too. Yes, that's good, that way no-one gets hurt, not mother, not us. If she or we should have a baby, let's believe it's the cabbage patch. And that's the way things that adults call 'old wives tales' are made and carried on from generation to generation.

But really it is about time that something different happened, because after all what we are asking for is the truth, the factual truth. Lots of our parents will say, 'Well, when shall I tell him?' *The answer to that is as soon as we ask.* If our parents were really honest with themselves, they would notice our interest in their giggles and looks at each other, their hugs and secret noises at night. They'd be aware that we notice mother's slightly bulging breasts and her thickened waistline. We even notice it at times before father does, but rarely before our grandmothers do. It might be best to keep our eyes to ourselves, when mother starts to wear different clothes, and to stop wondering why she feels so different if she hugs us. But we can't and so we ask. Maybe it's not directly. We might be showing an interest in birds and bees and dogs and cats or pet rabbits, but we are really asking what happens to humans. If we are three we should be told. If we are four we must be told, and if we are five we should be told for the second time. Each year that goes by we should be told again, told facts.

Babies are made by fathers putting small seeds called sperms inside mother when he makes love to her. These sperms come out through father's penis and get placed inside mother's vagina. Then they swim up into this special kind of bag inside mother and join up with an egg. This egg comes from and grows inside mother's tummy. Baby grows there. Then it's time to be born. It's when baby has been inside for nine months and is big enough. To get born it comes out through mother's vagina which stretches and gets bigger just during the time that baby gets born. It's better for baby to be born in hospital because it's more comfortable for baby and mother there. They are the facts and that's what we want to know.

The trouble is that even if we get to know the facts there always seem to be even more facts to learn about. We might know all about how babies get made and born, we might especially have coped with the idea of how seeds get from father's penis into mother's vagina. But what we really want to know is when we can get a chance to try this out for ourselves.

How to discipline your parents

I am not really going to talk about when it is all right to smack your parents but rather about the sort of difficulty you may see when your parents can't make up their minds when to smack you. But it was a nice little fantasy for a few minutes wasn't it?

I remember somebody telling me that George Bernard Shaw once said, 'The only time you should hit a child is in anger.' Of course Bernard Shaw was a bachelor and did not have any children. But I think what he might have meant is that sometimes children will make parents very angry indeed and that it is all right to feel angry like this and if they lose their tempers and hit you they don't need to be worried. He probably felt that it was better to punish you in this way when you were sure to know what it was for, than for parents to pretend that they weren't upset, but to resent it really and store up more and more anger, until it explodes at a time when no child could possibly see the connection between the offence and the punishment. In a way I think he is probably right. But it is interesting that that's the way adults behave when somebody does something wrong like stealing or bullying or even worse things. They never punish people until months and sometimes even years afterwards and they pretend to themselves that somehow or other this is going to be a warning to other people not to do it.

Parents really seem to have a lot of worries over discipline. Some of them always seem to smack and some of them never do. The ones who smack us over the least little thing probably haven't got very good control over the ways that they feel, but often this isn't very serious and just means that they find it easier to express themselves in a physical way rather than by telling you off, often in words that you really can't understand. With lots of parents like this, you somehow feel that they really don't mean to hurt you, although I never believe that it hurts them more than it does us. Somehow you get the feeling that they don't hate you and provided you can feel this, almost anything is bearable. Sometimes of course parents really lose control and they may be a little sick about it. This is probably a bigger problem for them that it is for you, and if you can manage I would suggest you get help for them over it.

The ones who never seem to smack you probably think they are kind and mostly I suppose they are. Sometimes though I wonder if they don't smack you because they are really too anxious. Maybe they feel that if they get angry with you then you won't love them any more and this is more than they can bear. This is probably because that was the feeling they had when they were children and their parents smacked them. Sometimes they even feel guilty about wanting to smack you. Nobody minds a smack, but it's awful to think that the people you love most may not love you. These parents obviously don't realise that we really understand how they feel, particularly about aggression because, after all, we are a bit closer to it than they are. We will usually make allowances for them. There is a lot of talk about free expression for children and in a way I think this is very good, but sometimes parents with even the best motives don't seem to realise what a tough time we have trying to control ourselves even when we are constantly told how to do it. If we are never told it really is tough. If we are never given a glimpse of the sorts of ways we are expected to behave, we get anxious and we try and find out in all sorts of terrible ways how far we can go. If we never find out, it's more than possible that as we grow up we may believe that there are no rules and that we can do more or less what we like and that in fact it is our right to do so. There is a danger that some of us may never learn what boundaries there are to what we can do or, even worse, that we may never realise that any boundaries exist. If this happens we can really develop into a menace.

On the other hand it can be just as bad if our parents are constantly critical and never let up on telling us what to do. When we are young we tend to take parts of our parents and sort them into our own personality. You can probably all remember the time when you may have seen a younger brother or sister about to do something that he has been told he musn't, stop himself and say 'naughty, naughty' and perhaps even smack himself. Or maybe you did it yourself. If this is overdone, when we grow up we are always worried that we must do the right thing, we often work harder than we need to and we are terribly over-conscientious. We may be inhibited and fearful of failing, but worse than that we feel that failure is probably all that we deserve. Sometimes if we have been told often enough that this or that is very bad, we will pretend when we are adults that we never had bad feelings of that sort. That is why some adults are so much anti-this or anti-that.

In a way discipline should not really be such a big problem. All it really means is that whoever is handing it out feels that their way is best, and most children are willing to concede that their parents know more than they do and to go along with them. But we do like to feel now and then that what we think is respected even if it isn't right, and we like to feel that sometimes we are able to make a choice in what we do without somebody compelling us to do so. After all when we begin to discipline ourselves we know we are starting to be grown up. If our parents asked us how we wanted to be disciplined we'd maybe get real courageous and say follow our rules. Rules like the way to discipline is the middle way, the path between being too strict and too lenient. We'd want this to be consistently applied, with parents knowing what they are doing and not keeping that knowledge to themselves. We'd want them to tell us why they want us to do things, and what will happen if we don't stick to the rules. If we do break rules we'd want the punishment to fit the crime. If we break a plate we reckon it's fair that we should pay for it (if we can), but we don't really feel it's right that our parents should make us wash the dishes every night for the next ten years. If we smash up dad's car we really need a lesson; being allowed to drive mother's car next day is only telling us to smash that one up too. We'd agree with Bernard Shaw even more if he'd said, 'The time you might hit a child is at the time he's made you angry.' Not next day, next week or even next year.

How to handle your parents when you twitch

There are all sorts of twitches in all sorts of places. Little twitches that just affect a part of your face such as your nose or mouth or eye, or quite big ones that affect your hands and arms and legs and sometimes even your body. Some of these bigger sorts of twitches are given special names by doctors. They used to be called a kind of dance but nowadays they are often called Chorea which is a sort of an illness. Lots of things get called Chorea. Not all twitches are Chorea, even though somehow most twitches kind of look a bit similar with the strange movements we make when twitching.

This is probably a sort of a clue to understand what all the little twitches are about. They get to look similar because they mostly have something to do with twitching out feelings. Usually angry feelings. Having a twitch can also involve making different sorts of sounds, from grunts, squeals and coughs to real words. Whatever form the twitch happens to take it certainly is a very difficult thing to live with. Often we seem to get more or less used to it and after a while it does not seem to bother us unless other children keep pointing us out and making fun of us because of it. The people who never seem to get used to it are our parents and they often seem to feel that somehow the movements that we make are directed at them. Usually they are. Often they are our way of showing them what we feel about them in an indirect sort of way.

So it's understandable that often at first they don't take any notice and hope that we will grow out of it. But later on they get angry with us and tell us that we must stop or else we will get punished. Sometimes when we are told this we really do improve for a while so that our parents will always tell other people, 'Oh, he can stop it, if he wants to.' But if our parents really looked at what we were doing they might notice that the twitches turn to frightened sort of movements. It's almost as if we are fearful that someone is going to hit us, or someone is going to growl at us, or something bad is going to happen to us. In the beginning this is in fact probably what we feel, so often the movements start at a time when we are unhappy or afraid.

These twitches often kind of tell things about what we are feeling or thinking. But you can only understand that if you look very carefully and use a fair bit of thought as well as a moderate amount of imagination. The movements tell through the expression we may make with the face or hands or shoulders, of our fears, our feelings of disgust and shame and of having our 'noses pushed out of joint'. We might raise our eyebrows in a question mark look; the twitches might be kind of snorts of fear or anger; they might be excited wriggling of our noses or faces; quite often the movements are a way of showing sexual excitement. These feelings come out in this way as a signal of trouble. They always seem to be a way we have of signalling—kind of like a mixed up morse code but without anyone understanding the meaning of our message.

Usually our parents try not to notice these sorts of signals, and by the time they decide they want to do something about it, there doesn't seem to be much connection between what way we twitch and what happened to us or how we feel. So by this time it is often very hard to get rid of it. Somehow even we really have to concentrate very hard to make any difference to the twitches.

We can't really do much about these twitches all by ourselves. We usually can if we get some help. The worst part is that often we get ridiculed, laughed at and criticised. But even worse is when our parents try to bribe or shame us out of it. Even worse is if they shock us out of twitching by things like threatening to 'knock sense into' us or actually doing so. This just won't work. It can't, because we only twitch more and so as not to get our heads knocked off we twitch our heads out of reach or duck away. No, if we twitch we need help—that's what we are really trying to say.

How to train your parents not to mind if you are wetting the bed

One of the things that drives parents up the wall is a wet bed. Now this is a most extraordinary fact if one remembers that all parents were once children and all children at some stage of their life wet their bed. Parents are much better than we children at forgetting. For parents the memory of the smell and feel of lying in a bed soaked in urine is shrouded in the mists of sweet smelling, cool, crisp sheets, electric blankets, hot water bottles and things like that. They build up over the years a lot of fences, or as psychiatrists like to say, 'defences', to close in painful memories. If we wet the bed their defences tend to be knocked down, even if only a little. Once defences are down out come feelings. When connected with bed wetting most of these feelings are angry ones. Instead of feeling angry with themselves (or perhaps with their own parents) this anger is directed at us—the bed wetters.

Some of our parents get really steamed up when they are made to remember their own bed wetting. This is probably because they had a pretty rough time with our grandparents. If this is so, our parents are going to be doubly anxious because then they feel they will probably have to get just as vicious as their own parents did and so they seem to try to pretend that when you are a baby, or a few weeks of age, you know what is going on every time you pass water or do poos. So you have to expect that as soon as you are big enough to be held upright, without your head looking as though it is going to fall off at the hinge that connects it with your neck, you are going to be 'held out'.

Parents expect that by this simple and time honoured act you are in a position to safely deposit your 'jobs'—both No. 1 and No. 2—in a pot. It does not seem to matter to them that the upright position is pretty precarious and a frightening one for a baby, nor that you have no idea what they are up to. If by chance they pick you up at the right time you will probably oblige them and their sense of decency, by aiming correctly. Each time you hit the jack-pot there is much accompanying glee, so much so that for ever after pooing or weeing are likely to be connected with the idea that there is something 'funny' or even sensational about these acts. These particular parents really only feel proud of themselves when they tell their neighbours, their friends, the postman and the butcher of your achievement. All they have to do is to hold you out; you have to defy all the laws of gravity, child rearing, modern psychology and common sense to gratify their need for cleanliness and control. By the time you are nine months or so, if you have not completely mastered the act, it is likely that even sterner measures will befall you.

You may find yourself tied to a potty-chair for hours at a time, only given your meals whilst your bottom fills in the hole that cunning furniture manufacturers leave in the seat of your high chair, or get woken out of your peaceful sleep every hour on the hour to perform your duty. If you always eat and excrete simultaneously, there is little doubt that these two activities will get so intimately connected as to make you unsure of what to do when or where.

As time passes and we grow, the day arrives when our parents decide that it is time for us to go it alone. They know by a magic formula that we are big boys and girls now and allow us to control our bowel and bladder all by ourselves. This is without the previous encumbrance of nappy or pants or the hindrance of a pot. Once it is up to you those months of training are expected by our parents to pay dividends. Woe betide you if your confused sense of time and place, food or faeces, top or bottom, leads you to wet or soil your bed.

Some of your parents will have been more civilised in getting you to the stage of being trained. This state is a time-honoured one. There have been years when it was expected that each child should do his duty by the time he was twelve months or so. In other decades people looked askance only at the child who was not trained by the age of two. Some 'dirty' people never expect their child to be trained (but it is better to not tell this to civilised parents). To be trained almost makes a child like a performing circus bear, or at a more domestic level the house dog. It is interesting to note the efforts that some of our parents put into training the family pet. The wry smile if the dog should amuse the dinner guests by widdling on the carpet, the tolerance with which the poor pooch's best efforts to make his master's house smell like a public latrine, are in distinct contrast to the reception that we get should we wet our bed. If you try very hard you can accept this distinction between man's best friend and man's son and heir or daughter and delight. Unfortunately you might try too hard, not succeed, and find yourself accepting a dog's life for your own. Wetting in your bed, on the lounge room carpet, in the kitchen tidy, the hall closet and behind the bathroom scales is what the dog gets away with, so why shouldn't we. Despite all this there is one consolation for you. The family's pet dog will ultimately get put out and all that can happen to you is that you will be chastised, punished or rejected but never put out of your home, even if you never get trained.

There will come a time when you will go to kindergarten or even to school. These are places where you are taught to be grown up. Some parents also regard these places as suitable training grounds. Teachers by and large can be expected to frown on children who 'smell'. By having themselves been trained (as teachers) they are acknowledged as experts in all sorts of tricky undertakings. Not the least of these is the knowledge of how to get a small child out of 'the habit'.

This leads us to our own part in all this. Doing wees is something we discovered all by ourselves, probably when we were about a few months old. If we are lucky enough to be boys we might remember the delightful feeling of spraying mum whilst having our nappy changed. Perhaps we may even have been lucky enough to hit some innocent bystander, perhaps that bystander was a cruel doctor who jabbed us with one of the seemingly unending number of inoculations modern science has invented. Girls are at a distinct disadvantage in this delightful game— perhaps that's why they eventually wet the bed less than boys. They don't really know what fun they are missing.

Having experienced the feeling of power that all children get when they can stop and start weeing it becomes a kind of contest. How to hold it in and when to let it out is likely to be the reason for that thoughtful frown. Some parents will interpret your preoccupied look as the beginning of some sickness. Others will see it as a sure sign of impending mischief, but most of them will connect it with something sexual. This is partly because sex is a thing that occupies most of them for quite a lot of their time. Also, when you get thoughtful and particularly when your bladder is very full, you may jig around, cross your legs, go red in the face or even grunt and this is then taken as evidence of sexual feelings.

Because of the way we are made we are not really ready to connect ideas ourselves before we have grown up to a certain size and level of maturity. Furthermore, because our nervous systems aren't really all that good when we are babies, the nerves can't carry enough messages to tell us exactly when and where we should let out the wees till we are nearly a couple of years old. Then is our time to really show what we can do, but this is not necessarily when our parents expect it to be.

Having got to this mature stage some of us may have missed out on our training. We continue to wet the bed. When this happens we become the recipients of an enormous amount of attention. Now this is often just what we are aiming at. If we have felt let down over the arrival of a brother or sister, if we have been sick and stuck into a hospital, or if mum has been away on an extended visit to relatives, we often expect to get a bit more contact with our parents. One way of doing this is to pretend that we are still babies, go right on wetting the bed, and make mum and dad change this, the pyjamas, sheets and even our bedrooms. Even if we don't really want this extra attention we are sure to get it by wetting the bed. It is possible that this evil thing, the wet bed, will lead to lots of extra love. Mum might think she has to help us with our bed wetting by telling us over and over we are a good boy, or mummy's best boy, and mummy loves us even if we do wet the bed, so why can't we show mummy that we love her just as much as she loves us by staying dry all night? On the other hand each morning might start off with a few harsh words about being dirty, babyish, a nuisance, more trouble than worth and so on.

Some parents find it even harder to remain in control of themselves in the face of this very obvious breakdown in their training program. They could well hand out a few well-directed slaps or get out the family's accustomed weapon, be it strap, wooden spoon, fly swat, cane or that apparently harmless slipper. If these measures don't work parents are likely to resort to bribery, which comes in various disguises.

A down payment each dry day, with a further inducement of a bigger gift at the end of a dry week or month, is pretty acceptable to most of us. We might get into trouble though if we forget about the wet bed and still expect to get the goods. Hanging calendars on the walls, filling them out with stars and other magic symbols, really fills us with pride at our achievement and at the same time make us so anxious to get at least seven days in a row that we worry about it till we wet our bed and off we go again. Should all this fail parents can still call in the scientist with his machines. By tying us to a bell, electric shock or some other cunning warning system they hope to trick us into waking up enough to get out of bed, go down the hall to the toilet and retain dryness. Somehow parents seem to get just as many broken nights' sleep and visits to the toilet and ultimately wish that they had never heard of that infernal machine. It is just as well that often the machine does work, so that both parents and we can settle back into a pleasant routine of sleeping all night.

Probably the biggest trouble with this bed wetting business is that nobody, not even the smartest doctors, seem to know what really causes the whole thing. There is no doubt that some of us get dry a lot later than others and although sometimes this has got to do with the ways our parents try to force the issue a bit, sometimes it's got something to do with parts of our nervous systems maturing a little more slowly.[1] Probably both of these things are important. Some of us will just be slower to get control of our bladders and our bowels. This in itself isn't such a bad thing, but when our parents get all upset about it, and angry at us because of it, then getting better and gradually growing out of it becomes harder and harder.

It really is a problem to know what to tell our parents they should do in situations like this, but if they can learn not to do the things they shouldn't do, it's a lot easier for us to do the same.

How to handle your parents (and teachers) when they think you are clumsy

Being clumsy is one of the most upsetting things that happens to us. It looks like being foolish on purpose, or anyway that's how it appears to adults.

[1] See *How to handle your parents (and teachers) when they think you are clumsy.*

Sometimes I think some books that give advice to parents really do a lot of harm. Especially the ones that say when your baby is such and such an age he should be doing this or that. Parents, especially if they never had a baby before, always seem to be terribly anxious that we do the right things in the right ways at the right times. They take particular notice of when we smile, and often think we are smiling long before we do, when all that is happening is that we have wind. They are also very worried if we don't grow our teeth, or crawl, or walk, or talk at the right time. They look up their little books and they see that we are not right on schedule and they begin to worry.

Sometimes if there is no real way to compare us with other children they don't worry so much. If we are lucky they may leave us to develop at our own rate, whatever that is. But even good parents like this are not usually left alone by other people. You can be pretty sure that there will be lots of others around them who will see to it that they are good and anxious. Of course, we all know that the worst offenders here are our grandparents who keep asking questions like, 'Why isn't he walking by himself yet? I remember that you were walking months earlier.' What they are trying to say of course is that they were better parents than our parents are, and the point usually gets across. Whether or not it's true, and it usually isn't, our parents start to feel uncomfortable and feel as if somehow or other they are failing in their job. When this happens of course we are the first ones to suffer, because we are expected to sort of hurry things up so that they won't have to feel so bad next time granny calls. If it isn't our grandparents then you can expect there will be a neighbour or two who will come around and sort of casually mention, 'Shouldn't he be talking yet?' They are especially likely to do this if they have got children who are about the same age as we are and who seem to be doing things a little quicker.

Of course we all know that there are average sorts of ages at which we learn to do different things, but it seems to me that the problem becomes not so much whether we develop our ability to do this or that as that we develop it on time. This business of everybody doing everything the same way at the same time is ridiculous enough when you just talk about it. But when you find it's official because it's written down in books, especially when they are written by people who are supposed to know such as teachers or doctors, it's pretty hard to cope with.

Another idea we have to look at is that some of our parents don't seem to give us any prodding or pushing to help us to develop. Some even seem to prevent us growing up, even if it is only a little bit, by never letting us do anything at all. Well, if this is the way they want it we would be very foolish indeed not to go along with them. After all who needs to walk if he can crawl or even just sit, and who needs to talk if he can point. Some of our mothers and fathers keep us babyish; they protect us so much that we don't learn how to protect ourselves. They don't let us do things for ourselves, so we don't learn how to do them. They might stop us from doing any kind of thing that looks dangerous. This is because parents get frightened that we might hurt ourselves. Eventually, because we are kind of slow to learn how to protect ourselves, we do get hurt, our parents feel guilty, make doubly sure it won't happen again and so tend to over-protect us even more.

If we do get to do all those things we are supposed to do the fact that we might be going to be clumsy children becomes more obvious, particularly when we get to do the sorts of things that adults call 'social skills'. When it's all boiled down, what this really means is that we should be able to do up our buttons, tie our laces and tie and blow our nose. If we can't do this it's embarrassing, but not a real problem—at least, not until we go to school.

When we get there it isn't long before our teachers discover that we just don't seem to be able to do anything properly. We can't write properly and we are always untidy and spill paint everywhere. Our books have blots all over them and no matter how many times they tell us we just don't seem to be able to change it at all. They can punish us or give us little stars on our books for tidiness or setting out, but whatever they do we seem quite unable to keep things running smoothly and neatly. Mostly we even write our letters and our numbers back to front. Sometimes we find it difficult to read, not because we are not bright enough or anything like that, but because we just don't seem to see the words the way they are written.

When these sorts of things happen our teachers often become very upset. Somehow or other they seem to need us to conform to all the other children in the class. They want us to be average so that we don't need any extra attention. Of course this is not really their fault because most of them have got a terrible problem trying to cope with many more of us in a class than should be there. They are supposed to get us through to the next stage of learning, in only a year, and if they don't, they and their boss, the headmaster, have really got a big problem. They have to decide either to keep us down in the same class, and then they begin to feel that we might be sad about this; or they can decide to put us up with the others although we haven't really learnt the sort of things that we were supposed to. It seems to me that this kind of system is only good if you are what they call average. (But then I think that is true of all systems.)

We might get to be clumsy if we have had a small part of our brain damaged when we were born. Often it is part of the brain that controls co-ordination and movement and also controls how to see things, how to judge distances and heights and sounds and so on. This damage might come because we get born too early, which is called premature. Maybe its because we have had a very long and difficult birth or maybe because we get to be 'over-cooked' or even because our supply of oxygen and food tended to be a little less than we should have had when we were still inside mother. Being 'spastic' means that part of the brain has been hurt, often at birth, and that this part controls movement of one part or lots of parts of the body. If one part of our body doesn't work so well the rest also gets thrown out of gear and we get to be clumsy.

Sometimes there are other things which worry us more than whether we are able to write properly or whether our books are neat. These are things like being able to run or skip or hop or jump or kick or catch like all of the rest of the children can. When you can't do this sort of thing there aren't many children who will want to be bothered with you. They won't let you join in their games and play with them or, what is worse, they will point you out and make fun of you. Sometimes you don't have any friends at all and become very unhappy. It's times like these when you need all the support that you can get from your teacher or your parents. Unfortunately what you often get is a feeling of shame and anger. Here it does not seem to matter so much if it's a girl who can't do all these catching and kicking things, but if it's a boy his father often feels that it's a sort of reflection on his being a man, and father will never forgive him for this.

What happens in the end of course is that we begin to feel embarrassed, and we end up seeing ourselves as terrible failures and unable or unworthy to be with other children. Even if no-one ever says it, we often see ourselves as a sort of dunce, put ourselves in the corner away from everyone. We feel hopeless and depressed and often we start to fail even at things that we really can do. This failing business gets to be worse and worse as time goes on unless we get some help.

The help we need is mainly that all people, but especially our parents and our teachers, understand us. If they do then they know it's going to take us a good deal longer to get to be just the same as other children, usually till we are ten or twelve or so. We also need help with learning; sometimes we just need to be given the chance to do things over and over at our own pace, sometimes we need a big dose of 'remedial teaching'. (That's pretty hard stuff to get hold of because there don't seem to be many teachers who can dispense it.) Most of all we need to feel we are good at some things and so we kind of expect our parents and our teachers to give us some praise every now and then, to support us and mainly to understand us. It's a shame that they are usually too clumsy to realise it.

How to explain to your parents if you keep having accidents

All sorts of injuries that happen to children are called accidents. Really it's true to call injuries accidental only when we don't know enough of the reasons for an accident. The more we look at them the more we find out there probably are very few things that we should call accidental. By looking at some injuries that occur often and at some children that get to be hurt, we can work out quite readily what causes 'accidents'. Instead of looking at particular kinds of injuries it might be better to talk of particular kinds of children—those children who keep having accidents. Perhaps it would be better to call them children that keep on hurting themselves; or better still, children that keep on getting hurt. That makes it sound more as if they not only hurt themselves but that other people and other things can hurt them too. They are not really accident prone, just prone to be hurt.

Babies are said to have accidents. I suppose that sometimes these accidents are, as far as anyone can tell, real accidents, but there are very few of these. It might be if baby rolls off the changing table that it is by accident, but what was happening to mother whilst baby was rolling? It isn't really enough to say that a baby should not roll or that we did not know that baby could move so fast, or even that babies are always so active it's hard to handle them, particularly if they are as slippery as an eel after their bath. No, that's no accident. It might not be on purpose or with the real intention of hurting baby that mother, or big sister or the nurse, or even dad, let go. It might be that the angry feelings that the grown ups are not aware of take over for a little while and keep them from thinking about how slippery the baby is. Just the same way, when baby is in his pram, and his big brother or sister come racing around on their bike, knock the pram over and hurt the baby, it can't always be said that it 'is just an accident'. After all, we are supposed to be careful of what we do with babies. Grown ups should know if they put babies outside that junior could well be having a dare devil car race with next door's junior and prams do get in the way. In the same way, putting the pram near the top of stairs means denying the fact that prams could fall downstairs, almost to the point of saying that the stairs aren't even there, when they really are. Some-times things even worse than this can happen.

Some babies are hurt by a kind of angry feeling of their own that gets out of hand for a little while. Some babies are even able to hurt them-selves; for instance, head banging[1] can end in babies hurting themselves. Again it is a kind of angry feeling, an angry feeling without a loving feeling to even it out, to make the baby feel less tense. This business of feeling tense is one of the commonest in most of us who are prone to be hurt.

As children grow a bit from being babies they usually get to be more able to move around. They learn to crawl and stand, walk and climb. Some get to be pretty good at moving around, some even get to be experts—experts before they are supposed to be. If they are only twelve or fifteen months old they are not really supposed to be able to climb over the front gate, and by eighteen months of age be able to climb a twelve foot high wire fence. A few babies can. We might look at this as being kind of reckless. It is. Most of us feel more safe if we can keep our feet on the ground and not swing around in mid-air without being able to feel something solid to hold on to. But some of us, especially if we are this kind of expert, don't seem to care; that is, we don't think about not feeling safe, not having something to hold on to, and especially not that if we fall we'll get hurt. Not only do children need to be pretty clever at moving around, stronger and quicker than most other children, but also they have to feel differently about themselves, if they are going to be reckless. It's this feeling that is probably the most important

[1] See *How to educate your parents about rocking and rolling.*

thing in being reckless. This means either not caring very much about yourself, or caring a great deal but trying to hide this from yourself.

We get not to care much, or maybe not at all, about ourselves if we never learn how to do this, or if after we have learnt we forget it. It is only possible to learn how to like ourselves and care for ourselves when other people like and care for us. If our mothers don't care for us we might get to reckon we aren't any good. If no-one loves us we don't usually like anyone, especially ourselves.

Being reckless might be because we are real 'dare devils'. We get a thrill out of climbing high, running fast, jumping, whirling around and so on. It's a good way of getting rid of tense feelings; it's also a way of getting an exciting kind of feeling—this kind of feeling will sort of do if no-one really likes us. Dare devils usually get an urge to do something and they do it straight away—they don't wait to see what the consequences are. There are consequences from being reckless, usually; even if it does not happen straight away, there is an accident, that is, we get hurt. But this does not really matter much if you don't like yourself, for you have no real feelings for your own safety.

Some children are clumsy. If you are clumsy it might mean you can't walk well, you fall over a coin or even every little stone. Maybe if you're clumsy you try to climb but miss your step or even maybe you get onto the roof and slide clumsily down from it. Being clumsy might kind of lead to having accidents or to being more prone to get hurt. This being clumsy might come from a lot of different reasons. It is really these reasons that are the cause of the so-called accident. These and the fact of not being looked after well enough if you are clumsy. Clumsy children really can't look after themselves well enough, so they rely on someone else to do this for them. But clumsy children are often not very graceful, they are always in trouble for breaking things, or because they often get to be very active. Because of these things parents sometimes get to be very angry with their clumsy child, try to disregard him at times, and at other times without being aware of it, kind of on purpose, take not enough notice of their child. This means the child can get into an accident or hurt himself.[2]

We really need to be protected from getting hurt if we are retarded. When we are retarded it means we don't think as well as we could if we were normal for our age. It is not that we could think better if we

[2] See *How to handle your parents (and teachers) when they think you are clumsy*.

just would. We plainly can't. Being retarded causes a lot of bother, especially when we are small. Bodies grow and get able to do quite a a few things, but we don't learn very fast, so we won't be able to do things without knowing that they should not be done, because they are dangerous. Things like being able to walk across roads and not knowing that there are cars that might knock us down, or being able to reach up to the stove and pull down pots without knowing that we could be burnt by hot water. It often takes quite a while to catch up with these things, so during this time retarded children get a reputation for being accident prone. It is not really accident prone, but prone to be hurt. We need to be protected from doing things like this, things that hurt us. One of the main reasons that we aren't protected enough is that most parents who are unlucky enough to have a retarded child don't like to accept the fact. I don't blame them for it, it's just their way of keeping their hope up, hope that we are really normal and can therefore look after ourselves. Only this kind of keeping hope up does lead to children getting hurt pretty often.[3]

No matter if you are retarded or clumsy or normal physically or even spastic you've got a chance of being tied up with what are called 'neurotic' parents. One of these types are the apparently solid citizens. They bring up their children by the book and try to make sure you are clean and tidy, always on time, careful with money and have good table manners and so on. They themselves behave in just the same way. Some of these solid citizens are really wolves in sheep's clothing. They hide behind their facade of conformity a great big secret. This secret is the wish to live dangerously, to be a mixture of James Bond, Superman and maybe a dash of Frankenstein for good measure (the female counterparts might be Marilyn Monroe, Tarzan's mate Jane and a portion of Jezebel). They just can't let themselves do it, but they can try to get you to do it for them so they encourage children to live dangerously, only they never say that right out in the open. It might come out like this. They tell you never to swim in the river because it's deep and full of snags, and then go on to say what fun it might be if they could have a canoe to go on the river with. Or they might tell you to be sure you ride your bike safely and then buy you a speedometer so you can see how fast you are going. Perhaps they might warn you against throwing sticks or stones and give you a bow and arrow for

[3] See *How to understand your parents when you are retarded.*

Christmas, etc. This way you never get to be sure what you are supposed to do but you do get the message of what they wish you would do. This message of living dangerously is not spelled out by their words, but it is by the feeling they put in some of the words or, if you happen to be very alert, by the glint in their eyes. If you happen to be a girl you can also live dangerously. Mother might tell you to be sure not to climb trees and then add that girls are really just as good as boys and so almost dare you to prove it. Later on when you get to be a teenager they warn you against the dangers of promiscuity and equip you with a contraceptive at the same time. All of these things get called accidents, but it seems to me that there is a lot of difference between slipping or falling over a cliff and being pushed.

The most serious kind of accident proneness in children comes in those of us who just want to die and set about getting there. Now they don't usually come right out and openly say they want to die. They might not even tell you if you ask them directly, but they show through their behaviour that they are trying to get themselves killed. This behaviour might look innocent, like climbing trees and telegraph poles, or riding down the middle of the street or along a train line or by collecting gun powder, or perhaps even guns. Lately a new way is to collect pills: sleeping pills, tranquilliser pills, sedative pills and a lot more. Sometimes these are mother's pills, sometimes they are our own. What makes it look different is that it seems that the most innocent looking behaviour always somehow goes wrong. The branch of the tree breaks or a car comes along too fast, or the tin of carefully kept gunpowder explodes, or the pills happen to get mixed up with aspirin or something equally innocent. It doesn't only happen once, but many times. Still it tends to get called accidental or accident proneness and things like that. It isn't; it's suicide.

Suicide is a word that most people don't like to talk about. Most have the idea that children would never commit or try to commit suicide. Even when children sometimes come right out and say it— tell other people that they are going to commit suicide—they are not taken seriously. People, especially grown up people, don't like to think of suicide. Death is a kind of taboo subject. Most people don't like talking about death because it makes them think of their own death. For children to have any thoughts about death brings people to the idea that these children are too young to know about it. There is a kind of wish that adults keep up their sleeve. By this wish they can always pretend they are still children and don't know anything about death themselves. It's this kind of thinking that allows children to cry out for help with their so-called accidents, till eventually they give up expecting to have any notice taken of them and go ahead and kill themselves.

It will probably seem pretty strange to most of our parents that having an accident could be a way to tell them something. In a way I suppose it is funny, although it isn't a very good joke. The one thing that we would like from our parents, I think, is that they didn't just make up words to describe us, like 'accident prone', but instead tried to see what was going on. They'd soon find out that really accidental accidents are very rare indeed.

How to understand your parents when you are retarded

You would think that when we fall behind at school or when we don't develop as quickly as some of our friends or brothers or sisters, it was really largely our problem. But compared with what most of our parents seem to go through, it is absolutely nothing. This is even though there are all sorts of levels that we might be functioning at. There are those of us who are just a little bit behind the average, and some of us, fortunately not very many, who never really seem to be able to develop very far, or to learn much, or to look after ourselves at all.

In many ways when we are as badly off as this it is probably better for our parents. Although it's a pretty tragic thing to have a child who really doesn't seem to be able to act or behave or think or feel much like other children, you could almost say that there are not many questions that parents can have, there are not many possibilities available to them in the way of special help and there are not many alternatives that they can look for other than that their child is and always will be severely retarded. Even then, however, some parents find it terribly difficult to accept what most of us might feel they cannot escape. When they feel as bad as this they often blame all sorts of other people for what has happened, not so much to their child but to them.

The first people they usually blame are the doctors. The doctors who looked after them when mother was pregnant, or the doctors who did the delivery and who were too slow or too fast or too rough, or the doctors who said, 'He is a perfect baby and you have nothing to worry about,' or the doctors who said, 'It's only a mild problem and he will soon be over it.' Sometimes parents will not really take notice that anything is wrong until we are going to school, and then it is often the teachers they blame. 'He was terribly strict, all the parents in the school were complaining about him,' or 'The classes are too big and no-one can pay enough attention to him. He would be perfectly all right if only they would spend some time with him.' And sometimes they don't really know who to blame and it becomes first this person and then that. Some of them, but not many, are able to put into words what they really feel, which is that they blame themselves.

This must really be a dreadful feeling for a parent to have. It is so rarely right, but so often believed—not just by our parents but by their so-called friends and people who really should love and support them when they have a worry like this. So on top of the frustration and feelings of being inadequate and hopeless that you have yourself, you somehow or other have to try and comfort your parents as well. You have to be tolerant of how bad they feel and of how this may make them feel about you. It's very interesting that the sort of parents who seem to have most difficulty are those who are more intelligent. Somehow or other they, and for that matter everyone, seem to be able to accept some sort of crippling deformity or blindness or even deafness. But when the sort of problem you have is to do with your mind or your brain, I think they must become too anxious altogether and they really don't seem to be able to work out any reasonable method of dealing with this problem. Some of them will never accept that there is anything wrong with us, and in a way this makes us very glad. We don't really want them ever to give up hope. It's a good feeling to know that they are always looking around for new answers and new ideas. The problems seem to come though when they will never accept what we are and they begin to expect more of us than we can really deliver.

When we are only a little bit behind it's worse for us. People call us lazy and say that we don't pay enough attention. All our school reports are the same. 'He could do better if he tried.' This is really not fair at all, because we do try and, although we need it desperately, we don't often get extra help or extra consideration. After a while of course this gets us down, and we become depressed, feel hopeless and even more inadequate and useless than we really are. At this sort of time we often really do stop trying, and our performance falls off so that where before we were managing to stay at the bottom of the class, now even that is too much. It is at this time that a lot of really cruel things are said to us. 'I know he can do better if he really wants to. He has got a very good memory when it comes to things that interest him or that he wants to remember.' The trouble seems to be that what we want, and what our parents want and expect, are not always the same.

Then of course there is the other sort of thing that can happen to us when our parents realise that we have some sort of problem about learning or developing. Perhaps because they feel so bad about it, and about the fact that in some way they may have made us like this, they protect us too much, or they let us do anything we like in any way that we like it, in fact they more or less turn themselves and the whole of the family over to us. From that time on everything that happens at home seems to be upside down. Our parents and brothers and sisters seem to do whatever we want them to do and do it in a way that we want them to. I suppose we would be terribly foolish not to accept all of this fussing, and it would be silly to pass up an opportunity to get away with almost anything that we wish. The only trouble is that sometimes this isn't really in our best interest. Often we seem to disrupt the whole of the family's life which then starts to collect itself around the lowest sort of level that we can manage. What happens in the end is that we never really have an example to follow and we never really seem to have anything to live up to or to strive for. The only sure thing that happens is that it isn't long before our brothers and sisters start to resent us and to resent the allowances they have to make for us. It isn't much longer before our parents are openly feeling the same way and then we are really worse off than ever.

Although in a way we are sort of special cases, the things that we we really need are the same as what other children need. We need love and consistency and acceptance. Sometimes our parents, because they are angry with us for the kind of feelings that we create in them, go out of their way to prove how much they love us, and to do this they are often very inconsistent and never really accepting.

As well as needing the same as other children do, we also need special things. We would like our parents to stop pretending they really know what is wrong with us, or worse still believing that the ex-nurse across the road really knows. There are many things that can be done for us if our parents will only go and get an expert's opinion about how retarded we are. Not only should they ask the expert what our I.Q. is, but how it got to be less than normal. Once our parents have the facts, we wish they wouldn't conveniently forget them. It might be convenient for them, it's never really convenient for us. It is a dreadful feeling for parents to know their child is retarded. Still, there are some good things about us. We are not all so different or so dumb or so bad. Usually we have lots of good points as well.

Maybe it's hard for our parents to see our good points, especially if they are very upset with us being retarded. Even if they kind of deny to themselves we are retarded and over-protect us and so on they still might miss seeing our good points. They really need to see them to be able to treat us at the right level. The levels we are capable of doing different things at might be very different. We might be able to climb and jump but not talk in a way people understand us. We might be able to eat pretty well at home, but not in a classy restaurant. Many of us can pass for normal in social kinds of things. It's getting down to working out problems or learning new things that kind of finds us out.

It's when we are unable to do all the normal things that we'd like not just our parents, but also our friends and teachers and really the whole community to accept us as we are. If they did it might make it easier for our parents—they find it hard enough without other people making them feel even more upset or guilty or ashamed. Sometimes they get to be so ashamed they tie us up and hide us away in back gardens or sheds and so on. If they have to do that we'd really be better off in a hospital or some kind of home suitable for what we need. We are kind of special and need help to try as much as we can to keep up with the others.

How to manage your parents when you are having convulsions

Most children who have convulsions do so because they have epilepsy. Epilepsy is a pretty common sickness, but it isn't the only reason for having convulsions. Most people don't like the words epilepsy and epileptics, so they call having convulsions by names like fits, turns, attacks, shakes or just plain 'it'. By using words like these people can hide from themselves the bad kind of feelings they have about epilepsy and convulsions in general. These bad feelings are always kind of connected with the feeling of fear, particularly the fear of death and the fear of madness. It's these kinds of ideas that people have about epilepsy, ideas of being unconscious or dead and of being afraid or mad, that really start to get hold of children with epilepsy. Sometimes these feelings and ideas can cause more trouble than epilepsy itself.

We can have epilepsy at all ages. Babies have convulsions, but usually it is not epilepsy that causes them, but high temperature or fever. Even so, little babies do have convulsions because of epilepsy, though, since most of us sleep a good deal of the time at that age, we get away with it. People don't get suspicious about us till later on. When we are sitting up, but more often when toddling on our feet, if we have a convulsion it's much harder to stay upright and we get found out. As time goes on it gets to be harder and harder on us, but also harder on our parents. They try to hide the fact of our having convulsions. In our early school years most of us who have convulsions seem to get them because of epilepsy and not any more because of fever. Epilepsy can get in the way of our learning at school and also, because we tend to meet a lot more children and people, many more people get to know about our having epilepsy. This gets to be quite a worry. But not nearly as big a worry as adolescents have with convulsions. It's probably at this time more than any other that having convulsions and particularly epilepsy is very frightening, very much connected with ideas of death and madness. This time, in our teenage years, is also the time when we are most likely to have convulsions, not because of epilepsy, nor because of fever, but because of mixed-up feelings.

The kind of convulsion we have can vary a lot. Epilepsy can be a little period of not being with it, a blank stare, a minor loss of attention lasting no more than a part of a second. If we have only a few of these, say one or two in a week, we certainly are aware of them, but no-one else might be. If these little bits of epilepsy get to be very frequent, maybe even up to hundreds each day, then a good deal of our time gets to be taken up with being unconscious. If this happens to us very early in our lives we tend to miss out on a great deal of what is going on around us. If we don't find out about things we might even appear to be very dumb or even get called retarded. This might not be true; in fact we might have very good intelligence, but never be with it long enough to use it.

As we get older these little periods of epilepsy are less likely to occur. Babies can have other types of epilepsy, but usually other kinds start later in our lives. It might start by just a funny movement that comes all of a sudden, a jerking of our head, or a twitching of our face or arm or part of the body. This twitching, if epilepsy is the reason, is likely to be always the same. We might all of a sudden, drop to the floor like a stone, and then quickly get up again and be perfectly all right. Maybe we might be in bed and get a few trembling-like movements or kick around a bit or even just wet the bed. All these could be epilepsy of a minor kind, minor but different to the little bits of epilepsy we have already talked about, because here some part of us gets to move about. With this kind of epilepsy we often get the idea that something bad is happening to us. Usually this feels as if there is something that someone is doing to us, we realise we are moving or have moved, but don't remember doing anything to start that movement, or even having thought about wanting to move.

Probably the most frightening kind of epilepsy we can have and also the most frightening for other people to see is when we kind of collapse, shake all over, maybe bite our tongue, roll our eyes around and even wet or dirty ourselves. In part it is the shaking and the odd out-of-control way we move, along with the very big difference between acting like this and being normal, that is so frightening. But more than anything else it's because we look as if we are going to die that people get frightened by seeing epilepsy like this. This look we get, as if we are going to die, really worries mothers with children who have epilepsy. But it also worries us. If we are there one moment but not the next and we can't remember what happened to us it kind of feels as if we might have died. It gets to be an even worse feeling, if, when we have this kind of convulsion we fall and hurt ourselves. When we wake up it's hard to explain to ourselves how we got to be hurt. It starts to add up that someone has done this to us and we get the idea that people are against us, are attacking us and soon we reckon it's not a safe world to live in.

There is still another kind of epilepsy that is even harder to understand, not only for people who see it, but also for those of us who have it. Here it might start with a sound like a piece of music or with seeing something or smelling something or even feeling something touch our body. There might be the urge to do something and go somewhere; just the feeling and usually an urgent feeling that this has to be done, but we don't know why. It's all very perplexing. After a time we might even carry out some particular kind of action. It might be a thing we do every day, like going for a walk, or it might be something unusual and queer, like running down the street screaming. No matter what it is we don't really remember doing it after it's all over. This is almost as if we are kind of automatic, doing things without our controlling ourselves. This kind of epilepsy might end up with the same kind of convulsion as in the last paragraph, or it might go on for an hour or more. To us the worst part is the partial memory of having done something without really knowing what it was, or of having experienced something but not really being able to be sure of it. This can lead to us getting pretty disturbed thoughts. We might think we are being poisoned, or that there are people influencing us, or even that there are machines or robots that are making us do these queer things. On the other hand we might get so frightened that we get too scared to move outside our homes, in case this odd thing should happen again. For a few of us this kind of epilepsy gets to be real exciting, something that we don't quite like, but look forward to with a horrified kind of fascination. It may even get so exciting it gets confused with the excitement from sexual activities.

From all these ideas about epilepsy it might sound as if it can have a pretty serious effect on us. It can. Maybe because if we have a lot of epilepsy we get to be dull in our thinking or very frightened, as I have already explained. Maybe it isn't just the effect that epilepsy has on us that's important but also the effect that we, as different kinds of children, have on our epilepsy. In some ways it's more likely that we will have epilepsy if we are inclined to be immature. By this I mean that many of us who have epilepsy are also less grown up for our years, less able to look after ourselves (although often it's because of the way our parents handle us because of their own fears about our having convulsions), but more than anything else, less able to control our feelings than we ought to at our particular age. The most important feelings that are involved here are our angry feelings. If we find it hard to get rid of our anger and tend to let it kind of store up and then at times explode out, we are more prone to have epilepsy (though not by any means is this the only reason for epilepsy). It is also more likely that we'll get epilepsy if we tend to be very impulsive kind of children, and along with being impulsive, inclined not to have much tolerance for being frustrated. More particularly we might find that certain kinds of things that happen to us almost always trigger off a bout of epilepsy.

It might be that we are sick, not only with fever; or maybe if we go to a certain place which somehow makes us frightened or even angry; or even if we are adolescent and a girl and have a period. Anyway, no matter what kind of people we are, nor what kind of things trigger off a particular kind of convulsion, we are likely to have pretty disturbing ideas about what is happening to us.

Apart from those things I have already written about there are a number of ideas and feelings that most of us who are epileptic get—in fact these feelings are almost part of being epileptic. They seem to come out even when we are very small and certainly as we get to be able to talk about ourselves. Firstly, we all feel there is something wrong in our heads. It might be a feeling of something moving inside or a feeling of some kind of light in our head, or a kind of electricity in there— it almost always seems to go on to a feeling that something starts in our heads and then like lightning spreads to other parts of our bodies. When we are very little, we just talk of it being a kind of dizzy feeling or kind of headache. Later it gets to be built up into a type of story, maybe like there is an angry bear or a giant who is inside our head. As we get even older these feelings are more likely to be expressed in connection with the fear of being or going mad. This business of going mad is really a way of saying we're losing control of ourselves, something or someone is taking over from us and is making us do things, and so on. Even later the idea that we are sick comes out, and it's often thought that this sickness is a kind of cancer or growth in our heads. No matter what way these ideas present themselves you can see they are pretty frightened ones. They are all somehow related to madness and to dying.

As well as us getting these feelings so do our parents, other relatives and even our friends, and at times so do doctors who look after us. Mothers are always quick to see the connection between their child having convulsions and dying. They then might react in a number of ways. If this frightens them very much they might get not to want to think about this possibility at all, and even go to the extent of denying the fact that we have convulsions. In little ways we all do this (remember I said we call epilepsy by any other than it's real name). Other mothers tend to be so preoccupied with making sure that nothing bad can befall us they will protect us and coddle us to the extent that we are no longer allowed to do anything for ourselves. These kind of ideas spread easily and you will all probably know of the many things epileptics are not supposed to do—things like driving a car, swimming, working near machines and so on. Some of these restrictions are, of course, realistic, but some are archaic and through their lack of making sense show they arose out of fear. This fear is common to all people who have anything to do with epilepsy. One way of trying to handle this fear is to lock it up. This is what still happens to children with epilepsy—they get locked up. Not because they always need to be protected, but sometimes because people are scared of epileptics.

Not all convulsions are epilepsy. As little children one of the things that gets to be called epilepsy comes from us holding our breaths. In fact we might hold our breath so long we go unconscious and even have an epileptic convulsion, but usually we don't. These breath holding attacks come mainly in our toddler years from the age of eighteen months till we are about three or four years old. Usually we have been naughty or got smacked, or we've got frustrated in not being allowed to have a biscuit or another lolly, or we might even have fallen over and hurt ourselves a bit. Then we start to cry and yell and scream and start all over again and cry and yell and scream some more. Eventually we hold our breath not just for a little while, but till we go blue and black in colour, till our eyes stick out and our bodies go all stiff. Just when it looks as though we are not going to ever breathe again we suddenly do. We might even start all over again and this can be just as frightening to our parents as a real convulsion. It can be so frightening they will do anything we want them to. This is what we are secretly aiming at with this kind of manoeuvre, and this is what usually makes us keep on doing it. Probably it serves us right if no-one takes much notice of us trying out this stunt. Certainly if no-one takes too much notice of us we soon get the message and don't try it again.[1]

Its a bit different if we should have convulsions because we are all mixed up in our feelings. Again, we want people to take notice of us, but even if they don't we usually keep on having this type of convulsion. It isn't really a convulsion but it certainly might look so much like one that it is good enough to fool the experts. Sometimes it's so good it might even convince doctors we really have some serious kind of brain trouble and they could even get to open our skulls to see what's going on inside. There are always a few clues that these convulsions aren't really convulsions. Firstly, they often look odd but not frightening, funny rather than fearful. They tend to go on for too long and occur

[1] See *How to handle your parents when you are having a temper tantrum.*

too often. They never cause us to hurt ourselves and rarely to soil our clothes. But most importantly, we usually give ourselves away by betraying that we know what is going on around us during the time that we are having our convulsion. We don't usually start having these kind of convulsions till we are adolescent. Mostly it's a way of solving difficulties in our feelings. Usually these difficulties are tied up with the way we feel about our parents and in particular over how we can show them our sexual and angry feelings. It's usually quite bad for us that we are good at having these kind of convulsions. We fool people and they treat us with extra special care and then we get to be in the position that having these convulsions seems worth while.

So you see this having convulsions business is all rather complicated and sometimes a little difficult to understand. Although I suppose when you really look at it clearly and see that it isn't all the same kind of thing, and that it isn't all bad and hopeless and frightening, it can become just another kind of illness. If you are lucky your parents will be concerned for you, concerned enough to get a proper what they call 'diagnosis' of what it is that is wrong, and won't be afraid to acknowledge that you have this sort of difficulty, either to themselves, to relatives, friends or you. They will find out and know that treatment can help and that we need treatment whether it's with some kind of tablets or with some kind of understanding, although usually it's both. Sometimes of course even if they try really hard to understand what it's all about, they don't seem to get anywhere because some doctors just won't explain it properly to them.

It would be nice to think that all of our parents would take care of us in this way, make sure that they know what is wrong with us and understand what it means and that we would get the right sort of help for it. As well as that it would be nice to feel that they weren't going to fuss too much, get terribly frightened and confused and make us feel agitated and angry and frustrated. Because of course when this happens, it's enough to give you a fit.

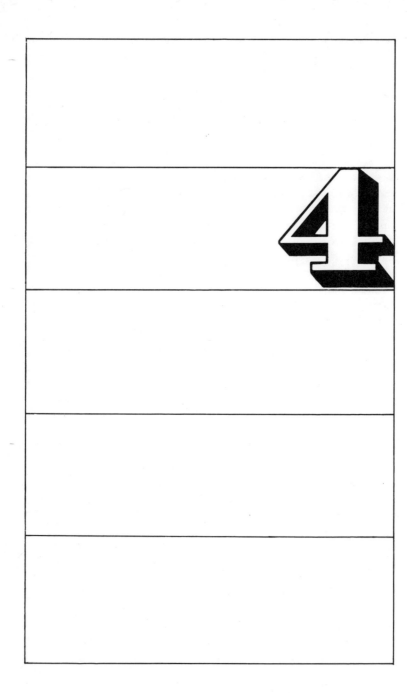

WE GO TO SCHOOL

How to handle your parents when you won't go to school

So you won't go to school. We'll see about that! You've got to go. The law says so. You're lucky to get an education. If you don't go you'll always be a bum. No nonsense, off you go—and that's what we usually do, that is, nearly all of us do. Every child I have ever heard of has said he won't go to school. Maybe not out loud, but certainly to himself. Some children find it much harder than most of us.

Refusing to go to school often starts when you won't go to kindergarten and could end when you won't go to work. Mostly our parents try very hard to find us a suitable kindergarten to go to though not all of them are lucky enough to find one. Kindergarten can after all be just as much a benefit to parents (particularly mothers) and it can be a help and a good fun place for us. Sometimes even when we are two or three we might be expected to go to kindergarten, although this is usually a pretty silly thing to do. If we happen to be four and we still refuse to go, then it gets to be a different matter. Not that there are not some of us at four who really are too young to go to kindergarten, but most of us at this age are usually able to separate from mother for long enough. Sometimes it takes a long time to get used to the idea. If after a month or so of trying, you are still obviously terrified of the prospect, I suggest you give up and wait until you are older. If you can get used to the idea of kindergarten and being away from home and especially from mother, then that's one of the best ways of making sure you will eventually get to stay at school.

For those of us who do ultimately make it to that important first day, it often doesn't exactly turn out to be full of fun. For example, you may never ever again see so many children crying, looking miserable, kind of lost and unsure of themselves, all at the same time. If you don't feel like that you're probably sick. It's healthy to have a bit of 'I won't go to school' for the first few days at school. After all, it's probably not the only time you've been away from home all day, nor the first time you've seen so many kids, the only time you've had to stick to strange rules or even the only time you've wanted to stick close to mother or someone else you know well. But it's probably the first time all these things have happened altogether. It's really enough to make everyone of you cry. That's healthy. It's also healthy to say to yourself that it will be all right, that you'll soon see mother again, that it's fun. Most of you will have been told for long enough that this day is going to come. All of you will have wanted to know what school is really like. A few of you will be able to go home at lunchtime, announce to mother that you've been to school, know all about it, you've finished with it and now you want to know when you start to go to work.

Some of you will be old enough to be at school, old enough by age, but not in being grown up. There might not be really much wrong with you, but perhaps you've always been a bit young for your years. Maybe you don't talk so well yet, are a bit clumsy with a pencil and can't really paint more than a scribble pattern. Usually you've been a bit slow to toilet train, maybe even now it's still hard to stop wetting your bed. Going to school might seem to be all right to you. Yet when you get there it's all very strange and very hard to take care of yourselves. You cry a fair bit, find the teacher is quite nice but not as nice as mother. After a while it gets to be pretty obvious to you that the other children are able to do their work better than you can. They can listen to a story without getting the fidgets, whereas you feel like it and have to get up to wander around. You look at their drawings and they are very different from yours. Theirs look like men, yours a mess. You go home and tell mother you miss her. She will most likely be pretty sympathetic, she may even say that you can stay home next day. After a while this gets to be a pattern—school for a few days each week, home for the rest. Soon the first school holidays come and after they're over you reckon you won't go back to school. Not being too firm about this you allow mother to persuade you to go just to try it for that day and if you don't like it you can stay home the next. You do. It's a dead end for you. Soon you can't go to school at all, not because you're sick, but because you're not yet developed enough to make it on your own. Probably you'd do it, but one of the reasons you're slow in developing is mother (and sometimes father too). She has aided and abetted your late development by keeping you close to her, not letting you get to be independent, doing things for you when you really have to do them yourself. You'll make it in the long run, but by then you will probably also fail at school.[1]

There may be some very real reasons for us to refuse to go to school, that is real reasons in our eyes and probably also in those of any sympathetic, understanding adults. There may be something wrong

[1] See *How to handle your parents when you fail at school.*

with the school and usually it's the teacher. Teachers are human. You might not always agree with that. Just as they might be very human and kind and tactful so they might be less humane, angry and intolerant. It is not often you will meet a teacher like this in your first few days at school, but you might. Maybe you will later in your school life. Some teachers are enough to scare even adults, and they do (usually parents remember how frightened they were of their teachers). If you won't go to school because teacher has really got at you I don't blame you. Sometimes teacher gets at you because you happen to be the only member of a minority group in your class and your teacher is not very partial to your kind of person. Maybe the other children at school don't like you because you wear different clothes or have a better kind of lunch, or even because they know you're a bit soft and they like to pick on you. They could make it pretty tough for you. So much so that you refuse to go back to that school. The only trouble is that you will find it the same when other children in another school do the same.

In the olden days when parents went to school they sometimes had to walk for miles to get there. These days there are very few schools which don't have a transport system to help you to get there. Sometimes these transport systems are a bit dangerous. The drivers might be irresponsible, you might even have an accident in the bus. It should be understandable if we get frightened to go to school because of this, although often parents don't think so.

It will probably be worse for you if you're not very bright, particularly if up till now you've been thought of by your parents as a pretty clever kid, only they never had anyone else to compare you with, or maybe they've kind of known you were retarded but have not liked to admit it to themselves. You get to school and find it very hard. You don't understand what teacher wants you to do, but even if you do understand you just can't do it. After a while this gets you down. You reckon you're even worse than you are, don't feel like getting any more proof of how little you know, and refuse to go to school. Unfortunately for most of you who are retarded, there is a long gap in time between your finding out you can't do it, and everyone else, that is, teachers and parents, latching on to the same idea. Usually you get to be called lazy and stupid or it is said that you could do better, if only you'd try. All these kinds of sayings hide the facts.[2]

---

[2] See *How to understand your parents when you are retarded.*

But the majority of us who refuse to go to school and who do so for such a period of time that it gets to be an embarrassment to our parents are really in a different kind of trouble. Not that we might not have those other kinds of troubles too, but we are the ones whose main trouble is being very anxious about separating from mother. There seems to be a kind of pattern to what happens to us and to why we won't go to school.

It usually happens when first we go to school, or after we have been to school for three or four years or perhaps when we are in secondary school, around eleven or twelve or even just when we are ready to leave school at sixteen years of age.

Having a bit of trouble on and off in getting to school is not unusual. Then, apparently for no obvious reason, school gets to be a terrible place. You might say it's the special teacher who you don't like or that mathematics got to be too hard and you can't face it. Perhaps another child is always attacking you or even there are holes in the school yard you keep falling into, and so on. At the same time each morning you get a mixture of feeling sick, headaches, tummy pain, dizziness, having to go to the toilet often and bouts of crying with much shedding of tears. The mention of school gets to be enough to send you into a fit of crying. Each night you come home and can't get to sleep because you worry about having to go to school next day. Eventually you refuse to go. Mother tries to persuade you to go, then she will beg you and maybe even bribe you. Father will stand clear for a while, then rant and rave a bit and even give you a hiding. But it's no good. You still refuse to go. Then they get the idea that it might have something to do with all that headache, being sick, dizzy and other kinds of things you've had. They take you to the doctor. It's possible that you'll get put to bed, treated for anything ranging from appendicitis to migraine and eventually you're allowed to get up. By now you can't go to school, not only because of it being a terrible place, but because you've got a physical sickness or anyway that's what everybody says, and this flares up regularly. After a long time your parents notice it's only on Mondays, Tuesdays, Wednesdays, Thursdays and Fridays (on these mornings), every evening except Friday and Saturday, more markedly at the beginning of the week and most decidedly never during school holidays. It often starts just after or just before school holidays.

This sort of trouble seems to happen to those of us who are special in other ways—immature and babyish, but often intelligent and doing well at school work, prone to be sick, but rarely very sick, nor having required a lot of time in hospital, always very anxious about being away from home and away from mother. Going to school has two parts to it—going to school and going away from home. It's always the latter which is the cause of the trouble, but the former which is blamed for it.

If you have this kind of trouble it's because being afraid to leave mother has got into a pretty complicated state of affairs. Not the least important in all of this is the problem that mother herself invariably appears to have just at this time. Often mother has been sick, worried, or plain neurotic. Usually she is very concerned about what is happening to herself, yet is able to camouflage this behind her concern for you. You know all this and it keeps you close to her. You stay close to her to make sure that nothing will happen to her and also that if anything did happen to her it would not be your fault. She wants you close to her for a variety of reasons and so she aids you in staying with her. You've both got troubles and both need help. It's a funny situation, but often the rest of the family are in a kind of trouble too. They all kind of have to take second place to your troubles.

There is no doubt that problems which keep us away from school are terribly urgent problems, and that if there is one thing that our parents could do for us, it would be to treat the whole thing as pretty important. Of course often parents on their own aren't able to do much about it, especially if a lot of the problem lies with them. But if our parents and our doctors and our schools could all sort of get together and talk about what was wrong and what to do about it I am sure that they would be able to help us much better than they often do. Sometimes we need real help in just leaving home, and we need to see that no-one is really going to let us 'get away with it', or that staying home and away from school is really not the solution to any of our problems. If they do let us, it usually means that they are just as anxious or even more anxious than we are about the whole situation. We don't really want our parents to be frightened by the sort of symptoms we get, because when they get frightened, we get frightened too. Being firm and insistent is something that doesn't worry us, so long as they are kind and understanding with it.

I think the ones who should perhaps get the most sympathy in all of this are the teachers in the schools. It's rarely the schools' fault, it's only sometimes the teachers', but it's always some kind of trouble inside us or inside our home that lies at the bottom of our refusing to go to school. It's just that school is a pretty handy place to blame for all our troubles and, more often than not, for our parents to blame too. It's just as well that schools are made of bricks and mortar and that teachers are pretty tough too, otherwise there wouldn't be much left after we got through throwing all the things at them that we do.

How to manage your parents when you won't stay at school

Most people call this truanting. It is one thing when your parents can't get you to leave home and we have talked about this already, but it is another thing when you apparently leave home but either never get to school, or get there but leave soon afterward. Boys seem to do this a great deal more than do girls. Some people say that it is because they are more adventurous or more undisciplined or that they have less control over themselves. I think probably that it may be due to the fact that over all boys are expected to have more difficulties than girls are. Although I wouldn't want any adults to get hold of this information, girls seem to be much tougher than boys generally.

Not staying at school is a source of tremendous embarrassment to our parents and they usually take a very dim view of it indeed, once they find out about it. Well, that is, most parents do. Some parents think it is rather funny and are more or less on our side against the school which represents a sort of authority to them. These sorts of parents are quite dangerous to us and it's best to steer clear of them and have as little to do with them as possible. Sometimes they even go so far as to provoke us into staying away from school; sometimes so that we can go to work earlier and contribute something to the household. Now we know that sometimes things get pretty tough at home but interestingly enough it's not usually in the very poorest homes that this provoking business occurs. It's often in the homes where money is used up, frequently on such adult entertainments as boozing.

Usually our parents first find out about our truanting when they get a rather nasty letter from the school or the truant officer who is a sort of 'big brother' who is always watching you. Our parents may then rush off to the school and say, 'But I didn't know that he wasn't coming to school, he leaves every morning and I pack his lunch for him and he comes home every night at the right time.' They pretend they are very puzzled by our behaviour and because we have embarrassed them they are usually very angry. Very often they will tell us off, or threaten us, or beat us, and this of course is very disheartening. A few of them will take us along to a doctor and ask him to find out what is wrong with us. Some others will go along to the school to try to find out what is wrong with it. Not many of them, however, really seem to want to know from us what the problems are and why we need to solve them in this way.

Most of us want to go to school, or any way we want to be where most other kids are. If we decide to stay away there is usually a pretty good reason and it is usually a pretty obvious one. Sometimes we have problems with the other children. We may be too big or too little or too fat or too thin, or our ears may be a funny shape or it might be our nose or we may be clumsy or anything at all that is different. Children don't understand differences very well and don't tolerate them much at all. If we are cruel to each other some of us may take it real badly and may not want to be in a place where we feel unhappy.

Sometimes we get embarrassed at school. This usually happens when we start to get a little bit older and our bodies start to change and we are worried or frightened and don't understand exactly what is happening to us. We don't like to take our clothes off, particularly when there are other children around, and so we don't come to school on sports day or swimming day. When we have stayed away once we get frightened to go back and so we stay away longer and until there is no going back, not till somebody forces us to.

Sometimes we stay away from school because we are bored with it, and this can be because our teachers are bad and don't make the work interesting enough. Maybe we are really too bright for it. Sometimes we pretend to be bored because it is too hard and we can't cope with it and nobody wants to help us or seems to care anyway. Most teachers are good and kind people and try to help all they can. But some of them are just as bad as some of our parents.

There are those of us who have a lot of difficulty in understanding some or all of our school work and although we try and try we don't seem to be able to make any sense of it. We sit in school and we get to be real mixed up or maybe get depressed. If we ask for help there is usually no time or no-one interested. To be able to wander through the streets or over the fields or to go to a swimming pool somewhere is then too much of a temptation to resist.

Staying away from school itself is, I suppose, bad enough, but the problem is that it doesn't usually end there. When we are truanting we often go with other fellows and because we are together it's easier to be a little foolish. It is when we are truanting that we often get into trouble like stealing and breaking into places and things like that. Those of us who can't manage to stay at school often can't manage to resist temptation and often get into all sorts of trouble. It's probable that most of you who keep on truanting are pretty disturbed characters and need help if you can get it.

Unforunately you can't always get help of the kind you might want. Neither can parents. Often when you are very disturbed all that your parents want is to get rid of you. Sometimes when you know this it makes you want to get your own back on them. Not going to school is one way of doing this. You know your parents will get fined if you truant so you keep on doing it. Your parents want to get rid of you even more and eventually nobody wants you. Worst of all nobody really seems to know what to do about you; even adults who are specialists in getting kids back to school sometimes don't know what to do. No wonder parents who are really only specialists in being parents don't know what to do.

I think the trick to handling your parents in a situation like this is to somehow or other get them on your side. Whatever you do you musn't let your parents side with your school against you. That is a combination that you can never beat. You will probably think that the best thing to do is split them so that the school thinks it is the parents' fault and the parents think it's the schools' fault. Usually because of the way that adults are, this isn't very hard to do. Nobody likes to think that anything bad that happens to them or anyone they know is their own fault, and they are only too ready to blame anybody else who happens to be involved. But this isn't really in the end something that works out to be in our best interests. It is better if they can kind of get together and hopefully make a sensible plan to help us. It would be nice to think they could work out why we truant and work off their energy by getting rid of the why.

Staying away from school is really only worth while if you get everybody worked up to the stage where they really are prepared to look at you and see what your problems are. But if you just become the centre of some sort of feud you may even find that you and your parents end up in court trying to explain something that nobody really understands, and then it's all for nothing and you might as well have stayed at school in the first place.

How to handle your parents when you fail at school

A lot of us fail at school. If we talk funny, are clumsy, or keep having accidents, if we can't keep up with the others, even if we have tummy aches or headaches or maybe tell lies or do poos in our pants, we fail at school. Not that we don't do our school work at all, or that we don't get pretty good marks in our exams, but that we fail to do as well as we are expected to. By failing at school I mean that you could if, everything was going your way, do better than you are doing. Some of you fail altogether, get nowhere with learning, some of you get a long way but don't do as well as you might.

How well we do at school depends on lots of things. One of the most important is this business of what is expected of us. What we expect of ourselves, what our parents, our teachers and lots of other people (society) expect of us. It's amazing how many different expectations you can get from these various view-points. You'd think that everyone could get together on this sort of thing. Almost certainly your parents will say you're not working hard enough, or that you don't know what work is, because in their days at school they used to. . . . Invariably teachers will report to your parents satisfactory progress, 'but he could do much better if he tried.' This is a kind of tribute to you, but even more so to themselves that they really got you to be satisfactory against the tremendous odds of your non-cooperation. It's kind of a way to get parents to pat them on the back by their patting you on your back.

If you happen to fail to meet any of these expectations, that is if you fail at school, you may be glad, it might be what you've been working for. Perhaps because you reckon it will get you out of having to go to school. Maybe you're glad because now your parents will show a bit of interest in you, like getting at you to work harder, or trying to change you from school to school. You could even feel glad because you've threatened to do this if you didn't get that bike, transistor, or to go to as many dances as you want.

However, most of us are sad. No-one usually likes to fail. It makes you feel kind of different, or perhaps that other children are better than you are. We all like to feel good. One way of feeling good is to do well, feeling able to be satisfied with what we've done, but more than anything else to be praised by others for what we have done. If you feel sad at failing at school you might think you are no good at anything. Not only can't you do your school work but you can't even read properly or play games or sport, or even have fun. After a while this gets to be real serious. You get very down in the dumps[1] and get to be only interested in how far down you feel. This then makes you lose interest in anything and everything, particularly in ever doing school work and so you get to be even worse than before. You give up. Some of us don't have to feel sad to give up. Maybe it's a kind of defiance. 'You can't make me do it, it's all your fault, you didn't teach me properly.' You fail, then you blame it onto everyone else. Maybe the teacher, maybe the school, even the weather (it's too hot to learn, it's too cold to learn). The quality of lead pencils or ballpoint pens, your parents, brothers and sisters, and sometimes, not surprisingly, the whole world, get to be the cause of your failure. The trouble here is that we might be right in some way, but never altogether. Only usually this is a matter where we don't see things as having more than one cause.

Of course there are all kinds of different reasons, some physical and some psychological, that cause us to fail at school. Sometimes a bit of failure is not a bad thing and those of us who are what adults call 'well adjusted' can even make this failure turn into a good thing. We might never want to fail again, work as hard as we can and never look back. Some of us just seem to get started a bit more slowly than others and never seem to get the hang of school for a long time, and then eventually it all clicks into place.

Sometimes though there seem to be real problems, like being very, very active,[2] and this is often picked up at kindergarten. If it isn't then you can be sure to be found out at school, not only because you will almost certainly fail, but you will also probably have wrecked the school, the teachers' health and your parents' patience by the time you have finished your first year. Sometimes being as active as this has got to do with some damage in the brain, but sometimes it's just because of the way you were brought up and the way you feel.

However, if you are a quiet little thing, but just can't really manage at school, it will probably take a couple of years before anyone wakes

[1] See *How to handle your parents when you are down in the dumps.*
[2] See *How to cope with your parents if you can't keep still.*

up to you. Then teachers seem to notice that you are clumsy or don't pay much attention, that you don't concentrate for long, don't learn to copy letters properly, scribble all over the pages instead of working neatly, and all those other things that teachers dearly love to point out. They usually blame our parents for this, not directly, but by saying, 'Mother needs to be a bit stricter with you,' or 'They don't help you enough with your home work.' Our parents of course will always blame the teachers and they usually say, 'She is too young and inexperienced,' or 'too old and out of date.' Sometimes the teachers and the parents all get together and then they blame the school system and say that there are too many children in the classroom, too few teachers, and not enough equipment. Of course all of this is true, it's just that adults always seem to miss the main point. It's not that you don't want to do well, it's just that you can't, at least not without some special kind of help, help to sort out which letter goes which way and which letter starts a word and which letter finishes it, and even what it means to add up numbers.

Getting letters and words around the wrong way used to be found a lot in those of us who are left-handed and were made to write right-handed. You would think this would not be happening any more these days, but it does. Sometimes we don't make up our minds which hand we really want to use until we are six or seven. Sometimes we never make up our minds and keep on using both, but you would think it would be really up to us to decide. Sometimes people begin to talk about things called 'word blindness' and 'late development' as reasons for failing at school. I suppose it is all right to have little pigeon holes like this to give our parents something to think about, but if they asked us I am sure we would rather be just called John or Jane, not John 'word blind' Smith or Jane 'late developer' Jones.

The best reason why we should fail at school and the one that is least often recognised is that we have trouble with our feelings. It's a funny set up if you think about it. School is a place where we spend about a third of most days, where we are supposed to learn so many different things (the number seems to increase at a rate that is enough to make us all go on strike), yet very few of us are given allowances for the way we feel. Many of us feel pretty good most of the time, but a large number of us feel real bad, sad, jumpy, or so frightened we can't think straight. We don't feel this just at home (where all our troubles are supposed to come from) but everywhere we go. This includes school. It means that we can't possibly help but fail at school. We can't do any better than fail because so much of our time is spent in sitting there thinking of our troubles that we can't concentrate on learning.

Now if we've got these kinds of troubles it's probably better for us if we try to let people know about them. This might be by acting the fool or being a clown in class, maybe we keep on asking for teacher's attention even if we know the answer or perhaps we have to go out to the sick room at least once every day. It's better if we do this than if we do nothing and just sit there and be quiet. This is likely to be looked at by teachers as evidence of our being good pupils. If we don't cause any bother and we aren't in any bother it's bad luck for us that our teachers are not usually trained to pick up these kinds of troubles we have.

Teachers are not supposed to be experts in these kinds of troubles. Parents sometimes expect them to be. Teachers are not really supposed to be able to treat disturbed children, and parents are not supposed to be teachers. It's all a bit of a mix-up for us children. We don't know who is supposed to do what for us. There is not really much we can do about it ourselves, except to complain. The trouble is that no-one takes much notice of us. What we need is a special kind of schooling, till we can get help with our troubles. We don't expect teachers to cure our troubles, but we do want the people who make up programs of what we are supposed to do in schools to know that if we have troubles with our feelings then we need some extra consideration.

Although I suppose it's pretty tough on our parents if their child fails at school, there isn't really much that we ask them in the way of help. What we would of course like them to do is really to find out what it is that is causing the failure, whether it is something that is on our mind, or the fact that we are just a bit slow to develop, or even that we will never really be able to manage well at all. Just knowing isn't enough either, we have got to feel that, whatever it is that is wrong, our parents accept this and will help with it and will love us no matter what our marks are like. It doesn't matter how bad we are, there is always something good about us and it isn't really too hard for them to emphasise all of the nice, good and wonderful things that we can do, instead of the dreary, dull and awful things that we can't do. One thing is certain of course and that is that parents can't really be teachers and teachers can't really be parents, but still both of them are important to us here and it would be nice if they talked a lot together and worked out different ways to help us.

If we have to fail at school to show our parents how we feel or what our problems are, it's a great shame. But it's better to fail at school than to fail at life.

How to handle your parents when you have an asthmatic attack

Asthma can be a pretty frightening thing to have. It is a bit of a toss up who gets more upset, us or our parents. Probably after a while it is our parents who get more distressed, particularly if they have never had any experience of their own which will help them to understand what it's all about. Quite often of course there is someone else in the family who has asthma, but at other times it seems to come right out of the blue. Lots of us who have asthma will have had a skin rash called eczema when we were babies and this is a very troublesome thing indeed. Mothers get very heavily involved in treating this by putting on lotions and ointments and bandages and sometimes even tying up our hands so that we can't scratch when we itch. When this happens of course we may get very angry indeed and we cry a lot and scream a lot and our parents can see how angry we are and often some feel guilty that they have caused us to feel that way.[1] This is very important in trying to understand what happens later on if we develop asthma. Probably the one thing that everybody thinks about when you mention asthma is the wheezing. This is a sort of a whistling noise which sounds a bit like a distress signal, which of course it really is. Although doctors seem to know a lot about some of the things which cause asthma, like infection and grasses and house dusts and the smell of horses and some flowers and some of the things we eat, many of them still don't seem to be aware of the fact that it is an emotional problem as well. There are all sorts of things involved here, in the way that we feel about asthma. It seems all bound up with problems about discipline and control and aggression and feelings of anger, and in many ways it is not too different from a sort of a temper tantrum. It's just that some children (I don't know if you would call them lucky or not) are able to have their tantrums in this sort of sophisticated way.

[1] See *How to manage your parents when you have Skin Troubles.*

Most parents don't seem to understand how we feel when we have asthmatic attacks although they notice that we sometimes have them when we are a bit excited, either about going somewhere or after just having come back, or that we get them when we are worried about things or when we have just had a fight with somebody, usually them. What we really feel, especially when we are small, is frightened. Often we are not really aware of what it is that makes us so fearful, but mostly it is fear that our mothers will leave us. So it's a sort of cry or appeal to her to make her stay. Usually later on, particularly when we begin to see the sort of effect that it has on her and especially if we find it difficult to express ourselves in other ways, it more or less takes the place of anger. You see it's a pretty hard thing for a child to accept that it has angry feelings about its parents, and of course it is hard for parents to accept this too. So that when we have an asthmatic attack, it is really nice and reassuring to know that our parents, and particularly our mothers, are there, and willing and able to soothe us and comfort us and let us know that because they are not afraid we need not be either. If they can do this when it's bad, and at the same time begin to allow us a little more freedom in expressing how we feel at other times, then we may all be relieved to find out that one day the asthma is gone and all we have left is a little hay fever. Having symptoms is more or less acceptable, so what happens is that at first all that we want from our parents is a little bit of extra protection, but after a while we may find what an excellent way this is to dominate them.

Of course asthma is a troublesome and sometimes dangerous illness to have and often you have to go through all sorts of treatments with tablets and injections and periods of hospitalisation, not so much so that you will get better, but so that your parents will not have to worry about you any more. On these terms I think it is not unreasonable to try to use this to your advantage. Worried parents will go to almost any length on your behalf and you will find that you can gain all sorts of concessions from them. You will have a special place in the family and will probably get a lot more attention than your brothers and sisters and sometimes more than your father, which will probably make him very angry. If you really use it intelligently an asthmatic attack can be a marvellous way to control your family and there really seems to be no limit to its possibilities.

Of course lots of the time you will probably be so good at convincing your mother that you need her that she will never ever leave you. She will be terribly concerned at everything that you do and will in fact make sure that you hardly do anything at all. She won't let you go swimming and she won't let you play other sports, she won't let you go out and she won't go out herself. These mothers are sometimes called over-protective, and probably a good word for them instead of mothers is 'smothers'. This of course is what really sometimes happens, so that one kind of suffocation is replaced by another kind. The big danger here is that after a while you will really believe that all the care and attention she gives you is necessary and you will never ever be able to cope on your own. Well, I suppose if you have overdone it to this extent it probably serves you right.

How to handle your parents when you get tummy aches

I think just about everybody has had a tummy ache at one time or another, even your parents. So you can be pretty sure that they'll take quite a lot of notice of you if you begin complaining of one. After all the tummy is a pretty important thing to all of us. When we are little everything that we think is good goes into and comes out of it. When we get a little bit older we begin to believe that babies get made somewhere inside, and it often takes a long time before we realise that they have a little container all of their own. (Sometimes our parents keep insisting that it is all done inside the stomach, and I understand that some adults really believe this.) Of course we are always very interested where babies come from and how they are made. If ever we get the opportunity we ask our parents and particularly if we notice that our mothers are getting rather large tummies, the sort of answers we get are rather stupid really: 'Oh, it's just that mummy is getting fat, hah, hah', or 'Mummy's got a lot of wind'. Sometimes I wonder if parents really think we believe that sort of stuff.

Often parents worry that if we complain of a tummy ache we really have got some disease inside us. One of the common diseases that all parents know about is appendicitis. They are frightened that we will have something terrible like that, and so they always rush us off to the doctors to see what he says. Unfortunately doctors also worry about this sort of thing and in the end they often take our appendix out, mostly when there is not even anything wrong with it at all. When they find this out they usually say, 'Oh well, it's better out anyway', or even such things as, 'Well, it didn't do him any harm'. Somehow or other they never seem to think of the sort of feelings that we have about being rushed into some hospital, usually in the middle of the night, meeting all sorts of strange people, having injections and things, having our tummy hurt like anything for days afterwards, feeling sick, and wondering why it is that our parents should want to punish us as much as all this when all we wanted to do was to tell them that we were feeling unhappy.

A lot of adults don't seem to realise that all pain means something, and often that it's not anything to do with any part of our bodies. Often a pain is a sort of a signal, for things that we want to say but somehow or other we aren't able to or we are not allowed to. Probably we would be better off if instead of saying, 'I've got a tummy ache', we said, 'I've got an "I'm afraid" sort of feeling', or 'I've got an "I don't want to" sort of feeling'. For example it could be 'I am afraid of going to school', or 'I don't want to eat the cabbage', and things like that. Somehow this seems a bit hard for our parents to understand. So when we find that this sort of thing does not seem to get through to our parents we try to keep it all inside until eventually it starts to hurt us, so much that we begin to complain about it. One thing that a lot of parents don't seem to realise is that it really *does* hurt us. We don't just make it up, or anyway not always. Just because when the sort of things that we have been worrying about settle down, our pains seem to get better, our parents sometimes think we are putting it on. But usually we are not. Even adults get all sorts of symptoms when they find things are getting too tough for them, and usually they only get better when they realise the problem is over, or they feel they can manage better some other way. Many of them seem to repeat this sort of thing over and over again, because it's what they learnt to do when they were children. They have of course the advantage on us there, because being older they have all sorts of different ways that they can use to solve their problems.

One of the problems that we sometimes have is when, because of the way our parents treat us, we find out that having a tummy ache is better than not having it. Often we find out all sorts of things, like extra attention, being able to do things that we are not allowed to do otherwise, and not having to do things that we usually do have to do, happen to us if we are sick and in pain. Our parents are more or less used to making allowances for each other if they say they have a pain of some sort. Most of you must have heard your mothers saying to somebody they don't like, 'No, I'm terribly sorry, but I won't be able to come out because I've got a tummy upset.' When of course anybody knows that they haven't at all. Or maybe that is not really fair. Maybe they would have a pain if they did the sort of thing that they really did not want to do, so they don't do it and then they don't get a pain. This is really all that we do, but for some reason parents seem to have difficulties in understanding it.

Sometimes we find we can actually use our tummy ache to manipulate our parents and even our teachers in order to get our own way. Lots of us get out of all sorts of very special things, like doing arithmetic. We are always running out to the toilet because of our tummy ache and pretty soon we are so bad in arithmetic that it gives us a tummy ache just to think about it.

Being sick is all right I suppose if there really isn't any other way that you can cope with your parents, or get them to understand the way you feel, but I think it really is a bit of a risk to keep getting tummy aches since parents have all sorts of ways of punishing us for that. It's all so simple really, you would think that our parents would be able to work out for themselves that when we have a tummy ache we would like them to ask, 'I wonder what you think is causing it?' or 'Sometimes when I get worried I get a tummy ache. Have you got any worries?' But as I have said they get us operated on, or if that does not happen they have us doing all sorts of horrible tests, seeing lots and lots of doctors who push us in the tummy and ask us what is wrong but will never listen to what we say. Sometimes it almost seems as if parents will go to any lengths to prove that there isn't any real reason for us to have a tummy ache, and when they do they just settle down with a sort of smug look on their faces and pretend that they have done all they have to for us. Well, if you are in a situation like that, you might just as well have a temper tantrum. At least they can't ignore that.

How to manage your parents when you have headaches

'I've got a headache.' It's said by mother and father, brother and sister, uncles, aunts, grandparents, by our kindergarten teachers and our teachers at school, by the lady next door and the man in the pet shop. Everyone seems to have a headache. Usually we can hear them say,

'Don't bother me, I've got a headache,' or 'Not now, I can't do it now, I've got a headache,' or 'Stop doing this or that, you'll give me a headache.' In fact, it almost seems that headaches are about as common as heads. Headaches are almost as frequent a topic of conversation as is the weather. We hear about them in our homes, down the street, in school and in church. We learn what to do for them by watching T.V. and in almost every newspaper, magazine or periodical you can buy. We get headaches, we have to. How could we be so different from everyone else? Maybe we don't really know what it means to have a headache, especially if we are only three or four years old, but we certainly know you've got to have a headache to be with it, to be recognised and to get attention.

Because everybody has had a headache at some time or other, as soon as we say we've got a headache, they immediately know what we are talking about. It's a bit like a form of currency, a way of communicating information. It's not surprising then that headaches get to be blamed for lots of different things. Headaches do come from a lot of physical things like fever, infections, head injuries and broken noses, heart disease and high blood pressure and brain tumours. But not all headaches are due to brain tumours, nor are they all caused by sinusitis. From the way people talk about it all headaches sound as if they are migraine. They aren't that either. Eye strain, overwork, fatigue, indigestion, constipation, late nights, 'the North wind', a bad liver are all blamed for headaches. They rarely are the cause though. Usually when we have a headache it's a way of communicating.

We children know how important headaches are. We have learnt that our heads are very precious. In our heads are our brains. We may have a lot of brains, which makes our parents real proud of us. They say, 'My kid's a real brain,' almost as if the only thing about us that is of any value is this brain thing. Or maybe we hear them say, 'Use your brains,' 'Get rid of that sawdust and try using your brain for a change,' or even, 'Take your head off and make it think for you.' We may get the idea that our brains are not much good or at the best no use at all. Our brains are inside a thing called the skull. We seem to either be 'thick-skulled', which somehow means we have no brains, or to be a 'numskull', which seems to be being stupid. Sometimes our skull is threatened with such words as 'I'll bash your skull in.' Rarely is it praised as being particularly beautiful or even useful. Somewhere within this head, brain and skull is our mind. This appears to be a rather funny sort of thing, almost a way of describing someone. 'He's quick minded,' or 'He is dirty minded,' 'He's got a good mind,' 'If he had any kind of mind at all he'd be a moron,' and so on. All this tends to be rather confusing. How can our heads be the part of us that is so good and so bad, so important and so useless, so necessary and yet so vulnerable. It's enough to give you a headache.

It's probably because our heads are so much in our thoughts (or are our thoughts in our heads?) that heads become the site of pain. It's not really as simple as that, but it's true that if we get into trouble, or if we get to be disturbed, we very often end up having headaches. Some of us are more likely to get headaches. If mother has headaches we can be almost a 100 per cent sure to get them. If not only mother, but grandmother (on mother's side) has them, we have no other choice. That goes not only for girls but for boys as well. Fathers also get headaches, as do their sons and their sons' sons. Does this mean that headaches are contagious? Not really contagious, just that they are not patented and so available for anyone to copy. They get to be imitated, headaches get to be one way of being like mother or father. We identify ourselves with our parents by having what they have, doing what they do. They have headaches, so do we. It isn't that we like to have headaches, but if we have worries that we can't solve, feelings we can't get rid of, we find headaches to be an acceptable way of expressing our troubles. If headaches are good enough to be caused by our parent's worries, then they can just as well be caused by our own.

This business of getting rid of worry by getting headaches is likely to spread to all kinds of worries. Some of us get headaches if we get frightened, some if we get very tense. These headaches get to take the place of feelings. It's easier to talk about having a headache than to tell about feelings. It's hard to speak of being very angry, of being so angry we could burst. Headaches are sometimes described as feeling as if our head is going to burst, not because of it being full of dynamite but full of feelings, just as powerful as dynamite.

For many of us headache is a way of kind of punishing ourselves. Headaches hurt. If we feel bad because of what we have done and thought, particularly to or about our parents, we might feel we need to be punished. Headaches can be like someone punching our head or like doing it to ourselves.

The big trouble with all this headache business is that it gets to have so many meanings it's hard to work out what means what. One thing it does mean though is that we are unhappy and in distress and that we have something to say, whether it's just about the way we feel, or that we want to be like mummy or daddy. It would be nice if our parents saw it as a way that we have of talking to them and did not immediately go and do all sorts of wonderful but terrible tests on us that the doctors think up, but just listened and tried to find out what it was we wanted to say. Maybe we would all feel better if it got to be possible for us to screw our heads off and get new ones every time we felt like it. But since we can't do it that way, we don't want our parents to 'bite our heads off', either. Heads are precious and we might even find some use for them one day.

How to explain to your parents when you steal things

All children steal something some time. We would not be children if we didn't. We've got to have something and we get told we can't, but we take it. That's stealing, isn't it? If you reckon it isn't you haven't stolen anything lately and that means you're probably what they call an adult. Adults don't steal things because it's wrong to steal. They've got a conscience, that's what stops them from stealing. It's funny to think that a thing like a conscience is stopping you from getting what you want. Stealing is trying to get what we want, but stealing isn't really much fun. We always seem to get caught, sooner or later; some of us even kind of set it up that we get caught, so we'll get caught sooner. Some say they never get caught, but that's usually because their parents don't want to catch them. Parents might even want their children to steal. It's bad luck for their children that the police don't punish some parents for encouraging their children to steal.

You could blame all stealing on to parents. It's all their fault. They won't give us what we want. We have to take it for ourselves. Sometimes we think we need money. It's not very hard to find money in most houses. Where there are people there is money. Some adults keep their money on them, some leave it lying around. That makes it even easier to get. By leaving it around they are really telling us it's all right to take it. Otherwise why would they leave it around? It's important, this thing called money, it's locked up in banks. If you work it's to get money, if you don't work it's because you have money. If you think about money, but never get around to earning it, someone else will always give you some. So it's really easy to get. The easiest way is to take it. It's easier to take it if it's kind of left to us to take it or not. It's the same with food. It's just lying around. You find food in kitchens, pantries, in cupboards, in the garden and in some bedrooms, shops keep it and so do supermarkets and so does the tuck shop at school. Pencils, rubbers, bottles of ink, fountain pens, bits of jewellery, watches, torches, light globes, scissors, dog chains and transistor radios are all left lying around. All easy to steal. There does not seem to be any guard over them. None of these things is ever locked up except at night time. We can take them, steal them, borrow them and never return them. We call these things our own. We might not ever really need them or ever get around to using them, because we don't want them. What we want is locked up, it's safeguarded, harder to get at than the crown jewels, but much more precious. It's love.

Love is like money and parents have both. Just like money they sometimes give it to us and sometimes don't. Sometimes we just feel they won't give us love, just like we constantly say we don't get enough money. Love is the currency that exists to make all our transactions with our parents go more smoothly.

Food is also like love—at times our parents give it to us freely and at others it's withheld. Food can tie us to our parents, we need to eat and we need love. We get to know that our mother loves to feed us. Some mothers feed us so much and they fill us so full with food and even force us to feed, instead of giving us their love. They say to themselves it's because they love us that they feed us. It's often instead of loving us that they over-feed us. For a few of us there is not enough food, not enough love and we feel deprived. We can't steal love, but we can steal food.

Usually we steal at home, at least we start there. Later we go to others and take from them. From our friends and our neighbours, particularly neighbours and friends' mothers. We can't get what we want from our family, from our mother, and we see what our friends are given by their family, by their mothers. If they have what we want, if they can get their supply of love, so can we. When we steal at home and if we steal from mother it's often from her purse, her special hoard of money, her favourite biscuit barrel. Why should her money be saved for the milkman, or to pay the gas bill when she should really give it to us? It's more ours than theirs and so we steal it. Fathers keep a number of coins. They are new, but in ten years time they will be valuable. We can't wait for ten years, now is when we need love. To need something and to wait for that need to be satisfied is to be an adult, but we are children. What we want we want now, not tomorrow, not next week. Sure, we have to learn to wait, to put up with being without love, to realise it will eventually come. Only we can't wait for very long. If it's promised we can wait till the allotted time. Time comes and goes without the promise being kept, so we have to take it now, because we feel it will never come. If it never comes we would feel sad. We can't afford to feel sad because that's a terrible feeling. Not only could we feel sad, but also empty and unwanted and unloved. Especially unloved.[1]

Maybe we see that our brothers and sisters get what we don't. Maybe we are one of the jealous kind and maybe it's not really that they get more than we do, it's just that we think they do. How can we make up for them having more? Only by taking from them. Take things, their things. We must share, that's what we are told. It's good to share; you can't be greedy, that's bad. But sharing means only having half or a third, or maybe only a tenth. This is higher mathematics, it doesn't fit in with needing something real bad. Mathematics is logical to grown ups. All or nothing is the logic we use. We do have to be greedy. We are all greedy. We grow up knowing the feeling of greed because it's part of us. It doesn't really come to us, it's always with us. Our greed might lead us to take from our family; if our greed is great it will make us take from our friends, our school mates and our enemies. We often envy our enemies, that's what makes them enemies. They have what we cannot get. They seem to have more, much more and so we steal. After all, we were told to share and that it is a good thing. If they won't share with us and we do so much want to share their good fortune in having, we will probably steal.

Once we steal we are faced with a problem. What do we do next. We can't feel good. We did not really get what we wanted and we looked for a substitute, but it doesn't satisfy. If it's food we eat it, if it's money we spend it and then eat. We feel full for a while and then the emptiness comes back. Soon we hide what we steal, we store it up in a secret place. We know it's there, if we want to we can go and get it. We can think about it and hope to feel good by thinking, but we don't. So we steal more and build up the store but we still feel empty. So we sell what we have stolen to get money and we might trade for food. Then again

[1] See *How to handle your parents when you are down in the dumps.*

we eat. We feel empty. So we try to buy what we need. We tell mother or father that if they are short of money we will give them a loan, better still we'll just give them all we've got. Thank you, they say, you are so good. So we feel good. But maybe they don't get the message. They still don't give us what we want. Searching elsewhere makes good sense. We take our money to school, we buy food for our friends, we even give them money, they say thank you but don't buy anything in return, or maybe don't really share theirs out equally. They are greedy too. After all they are children.

What does all this get us ? We sometimes see all we can get is trouble. Mother and father are mad with us and that's pretty uncomfortable. Sometimes it's better that they are mad with us than if they give us nothing. So we learn to set it up. We only steal when we know that we'll be caught—it's easy to make sure. We tell brother or sister what we've done, especially when we know they'll tell mother or father. It's more subtle to steal money, buy a new pen and take it home with us. Parents seem to know about everything we own and anything new is sure to create suspicion. They get at us and we're in trouble. To be even more clever about the whole thing we might try to divert suspicion away from ourselves by giving what we have stolen to little brother or sister. We set it up just as surely because we know that our parents know that our brother or sister could not have done it. Usually we can create just enough doubt in mother's or father's mind to make the whole process quite drawn out. Till they settle their doubts in their minds takes time and often more evidence. In that time they watch us. We have their attention. We've got what we want.

It's worse for us if we feel real bad about what we've done, if we feel we should not have, if we feel guilty or ashamed, in fact if we start to develop a conscience as most adults have. Feeling guilty can make us get pretty disturbed. It kind of acts like a trigger to us. We might have to do all sorts of things to try to get rid of that feeling of guilt. We might have to get a headache, a pain in our abdomen or to pass water very often, or we might get to be pretty bad tempered, to get to wander away from home or even to steal some more. It's all really a way of getting punished, but punished by ourselves for having stolen something we wanted, wanted but did not get.

Not all of us who steal feel guilty, and not all of us have much of a problem about what we do with our stolen goods, nor are we very concerned about really being greedy. Some of us are very disturbed.

We don't reckon that anything is of much value, that it doesn't make any difference whom anything belongs to. It's just as well ours as it is theirs. We steal, we eat, we work, we play, we go to school and we truant. It's all the same. We don't love. Not that we might not want love but that we want food, money, toys, books, transistor radios, electric trains, cars and aeroplanes, just as much as we want love. It makes no real difference what we get and what we don't get. We're the thieves of today and the criminals of tomorrow.

Most of us, however, do place a value on things and most of all on ourselves and our need to feel loved. When we are going through this difficult sort of phase in which we feel that we aren't getting enough of the thing that we want most, it would be a help if we thought our parents would try and see beyond the sorts of obvious things that we do. Getting our parents' attention by seeming bad is not really our choice. It's just that it seems to be the only thing to do. It would help us a lot if they did not keep tempting us by leaving all that stuff lying around and by placing such a lot importance and value on their money and possessions. After all, the thing that we place most value on is love and I don't think it's too childish to think that that's what our parents feel as well. If we do happen to steal I think it would help us for our parents to be realistic about it, and to face up to it and to make us face up to it as well. To show us that we have to repay in some way things that we take and things that we do, but it is so much easier to face up to our responsibility when we know our parents are facing up to theirs.

Not all of us who steal are thieves and not all of us will get to be criminals. It's more or less up to our parents—it's up to them to see that we are stealing and not to condone it. It's up to them to see why we are stealing and to rectify it. What we steal is love and that's what we want. It's better to be a loved ex-thief, than to be a 'thief of love', for the rest of our lives.

How to explain the situation to your parents when they catch you telling lies

Telling lies is not something that comes naturally to us children. We have to learn it, and usually don't learn it for quite a few years. This is something that parents will seldom acknowledge, because as far back as they can remember we have supposedly been telling lies. When we first start to talk of course we often don't have the right words to express ourselves, and so we might use the wrong words and because our parents don't understand us better, they think we are doing it on purpose. Sometimes they laugh at it, like when we call every man that we see daddy. This is because in the beginning daddy is the only word we know to use for a man.

Another thing that our parents don't seem to understand is that for a long time we don't really know what the world is like. It is hard for us when we are little to be sure exactly what is what and who is who. Sometimes the things that we hear in fairy tales and stories, and sometimes things that we think about and dream about, all get mixed up with what is actually happening to us, or what we actually see. So we tell them things that we really believe to be true, but which they know are not. Because they know it they think that we know it too, and so they say we are telling lies. If they can't bear to think that their little boy or girl is telling lies, they say we are telling fibs.

It is really quite hard to learn how to lie. It is even harder to be a good liar. The only way we can really learn to do this is by listening to what our parents do. Sometimes we learn as we grow up that there are all sorts of good reasons for lying, or anyway reasons which seem good to the person who is telling the lie. When we are little, we might find it difficult to understand this. But after a while we find how useful a thing this is to know about and so we pick it up and use it too. When our parents really tell a lie it is usually to get out of something, although sometimes it is to impress people and more rarely because they are afraid. With us, probably the commonest reason is the last one. If we learn that to tell the truth is likely to bring us some sort of unhappiness, then we try to find some other way to deal with the situation. When we know we are going to be punished for doing something, parents should not really blame us for trying to get away with it. Usually when our parents are very strict, and we know they won't listen to any explanations, then we are more likely to lie to them. Sometimes though, we will tell lies so as to attract our parents' attention. This is of course a very unhappy situation, because we know that we have only got them to listen to us by a sort of trick, so we know that they really don't mean to listen and that we are really no better off. At times it can get even worse. We can get so confused by all the different things that we say that we really can't tell any more what is true and what is not. Our parents of course end up in the same predicament and they might get confused and worried as well. If we don't get somebody to help us, it may be that we will be telling lies or thinking lies all the time, sometimes even when it doesn't do us any good at all.

You can learn that there are different sorts of ways to tell a lie. One of the easiest is just sort of to exaggerate things a little bit. Sometimes you can do this so that people will think you are important, or so that your parents will be especially proud of you. Sometimes you can do it with other children so they will think that there is something very special about you or your parents, and so that perhaps they will even think that you are a special sort of person. Sometimes we have to make up lies to cover up other things we have done, that we don't want our parents to know about. This is like staying away from school to play or go fishing or something like that. Probably the simplest sort of lying is just to say the opposite to what the truth is. Funnily enough, it's the one that usually succedes best.

Adults say, 'If you are going to be a liar, be a good one.' Some of us really get to be 'good liars'. It might start just as we've said, because our parents are 'good liars'. But it might be that we are what is called by some people 'bad' children. Those of us who are bad might have got that way for lots of reasons, especially through having been in trouble over not getting on well with our parents. That's not only our fault, it's just that we're smaller so it's easier to blame us than to say our parents are 'bad people'. Telling lies is very much part of being a disturbed child. So if you happen to be a 'very good liar' watch out because you're probably good and disturbed as well. That usually puts you in a class all by yourselves. You really need more help than if you are just a 'good liar'.

We'd none of us really like to get to be real bad or real big liars. It's up to our parents to make sure we aren't. Maybe they'd form a union just amongst themselves which they could call the 'Telling The Truth' union. Perhaps they could charge stiff entrance fees, which they would forfeit if they told lies. Most people like telling lies but nearly all adults like money more. If they didn't tell us lies, always told the truth, then we'd never learn how to use lies. We'd still learn about lying—that's as I've said before about the same as learning to talk; but we wouldn't find any benefit from it. Maybe, also, our parents could be consistent in telling us the truth and in stopping us from telling lies. Sometimes they tell a lie in front of us and later on when we bring it up, especially if anyone else is around, they call us a liar. If parents lie they should be able to accept responsibility for their own lie. If they can so can we.

None of us really wants to lie, if we think that telling the truth is a safe thing to do. So when your parents ask, 'Why do you tell lies all the time ?', the only way you can really answer them is to say, 'Because it's easier.' They might be prepared to go along with that, but what they never seem able to accept is that they are the ones that made it easier for you. Parents try not to believe it, but there really is no such thing as 'born liars'. They are made.

How to understand your parents' attitude when you break things

When we are very little, we tend to break a lot of things. Usually we don't mean to, and it comes about because we are inquisitive. When we begin to see and feel and hear properly, we reach out for things and explore them with our mouths and our eyes and our hands. While we are doing this we push and pull and bang without really thinking whether we are supposed to or not. When we are that little most of our parents will accept that we have to do this, and will let us play more or less in any way that we like. Of course they have provided a sort of a safeguard for themselves, in that most of the toys they give us when we are little are made of plastic and don't break easily. But even though we just play some parents don't seem to be able to restrain themselves from telling us that we are bad. 'Naughty, naughty' is the way they usually put it.

As we get a little bit older, our parents tend to get more difficult to manage if we happen to break something which they have given us. They don't seem to know or understand that if we really enjoy a particular object we will often have to handle it and use it and get inside of it before we are really content. They seem to think this is being ungrateful—in a way meaning that we don't really love them or appreciate them. If they get really angry with us, they punish us by buying us lots of nice toys, but then saying, 'You are obviously not old enough to know the value of things.' Then what they often do is take all the nice toys and lock them away in a cupboard. The biggest surprise of all comes from how startled they are when they find us trying to break open the cupboard.

It seems to take us a long time to understand that the sorts of things we are given are not just pieces of wood or metal or plastic or rubber, but seem to have some special sort of power over adults. Maybe not all

adults but certainly over our parents. As soon as we begin to realise
how valuable these things are to our parents, we find that we have a
very valuable weapon in our hands. Even when we can't tell them how
discontented or unhappy or frustrated we are, we can show them we can
break things. This is especially effective when they keep giving us
presents instead of giving us love or affection, or when they use
presents to bribe us to do something that we would do anyway, if they
asked us the right way.

Sometimes of course some of the fault is in the sorts of toys we get.
Most of them don't seem to be made to be played with. They are
sort of mechanical 'monsters' that are made to look lovely and beautiful
and attractive in the toy shop so that our parents, and sometimes even
we, get taken in by them. The worst ones are those that we can't handle
or explore or enjoy properly. The ones we can't put in our mouths or
pull apart or see inside. The ones with sharp edges that can cut us, or
levers we can't manipulate, or instructions that we can't read, or keys
that we can't turn, or ones that will move the way they want to and
not the way we want them to. Of course the people who make toys
know that children don't buy them so I suppose they can't really be
blamed for making the sorts of toys that adults enjoy. Still I think it's
a bit selfish of our parents because a lot of the time not only do they
buy the toys but they play with them as well, especially things like
train sets.

Mind you, toys aren't the only things that we destroy. There are
tables and chairs and clothes, either our own or our parents but mostly
our mother's. This happens usually when we are really angry and we
feel we have just got to show somehow or other the way that we feel.
When this happens we choose the sorts of things that we think will
mean the most to her. Sometimes this is her dresses or sometimes if we
can't get to them it is our dresses or pants. When things have gone this
far it's probably time to get your parents to take you to the doctors.
They probably will because they will be so angry with you.

Probably the worst thing about the way we destroy things is that we
seem to bring something to our parents' attention that some of them
really don't want to know about. This is of course the sorts of angry
feelings that they have inside themselves, but that they have gone to
great trouble to disguise in different sorts of ways over a very long time.
Mostly adults do such a good job over this that they end up thinking
that these sorts of feelings are just not there at all. They get terribly

angry when they are reminded that they are, and will go to almost any lengths to continue this sort of 'pretend game' that they play.

The ways that they really feel deep inside, though, come out when they are not altogether on their guard—like when they drink too much, or when they get very excited, or sometimes when something makes them so angry that they just can't control themselves any more. I understand this sometimes happens when they are talking about things like politics or religion or hanging.

In a way I suppose it must be frightening to some of our parents to see us as a sort of mirror. We reflect their own feelings that are sort of frightening to them. Sometimes this will be so bad that they might even provoke us into being destructive, so that then they can punish us and somehow or other this makes them feel better and safe about their own feelings. I don't want you to get the idea that I am saying that all of us children are terribly good and we are not naturally aggressive, because we are, right from the beginning. But we are not usually hypocritical or vindictive or bigoted. These are different kinds of refinements that we add on as we get to be adults. Usually we can see our parents' attitude to our breaking things. Sometimes we can even understand it. But only very rarely can we do anything about it ourselves. If only our parents would realise that they need to help us with this breaking business, then we might be able to stop. Maybe we would not even start to break things. We shouldn't if we got to learn a worthwhile way of working out what's valuable and what's not. Most parents seem to think everything is so valuable they never have anything that's just good for breaking up. But there are a few parents who don't value anything except their car, refrigerator (which is usually empty), television set and their portable can opener. Somewhere between these two kinds of attitudes is a way of knowing what's so valuable we shouldn't break it and what's fair game for our destructive urges. If we could find out this rule then we could probably also learn what we should look after ourselves. We'd learn that we should be responsible for our own things and that other people are supposed to be the same for their things. But this would only work if adults put the things they really like in a safe place. Otherwise, they are kind of inviting us to break them up, especially when breaking up things is our way of getting at our parents. Our way of getting angry with them without showing them right out in the open that we are angry with them.

When we do get so angry, we need more than at most other times to have our parents near us. That's so you can hit them or hurt them, you'll say. Well, in a way it is. But really it's to get them to hold on to you; to stop you from letting those very angry feelings break something or hurt somebody. We like this, we like to have our parents stop us and hold us and support us, till we kind of feel less angry and can stop ourselves and hold in our angry feelings ourselves. This way of sorting those angry feelings out so that we can let them out at the right time and in a reasonable kind of way is the kind of refinement we would really like to add on as we get to be adults. Anyway breaking up the furniture isn't really as bad as 'breaking up a home', which is something adults often seem to do.

How to explain to your parents when they discover you are being a bully

Being a bully is when you take advantage of how big you are to control those who are littler. This is, of course, what our parents are doing all the time. In fact, it seems to me that adults do this sort of thing all their lives, either to other adults, or, if a lot of them get together in what they call a group, to other littler groups or even to other littler countries. So you see although parents would never admit it, they are probably bigger bullies than we are.

All of this is very important when trying to understand how we become bullies in the first place. When we are very little, the first real thought that we get to know or to understand is that the most important things to us are controlled by people who are much bigger than we are. At the beginning it is only what we eat, but we find out that these huge things that lift us up and feed us and, if we are lucky, cuddle and love us, have the last word in what we eat and when we eat. Sometimes they don't take any notice of whether we are hungry or not, but they feed us at certain set times of the day. This is because it suits them better and in a way I don't suppose we can blame them for that. However, it sometimes makes us very angry indeed, and we feel inside as if we would like to do something terrible to them. What worries us is that we are powerless to alter the way they behave, and this makes us pretty frightened.

This sort of feeling is a very important one, and once we have learnt it we are not likely to forget it. In case we do our parents have all sorts of other opportunities for showing us that they are the boss.

When we are a little bit older, and the battles over what we are going to eat or whether we are going to eat are more or less finished, we often fight them over whether or not we are going to do our poos, and when and where. This is probably the first time that we realise that we may have a sort of advantage over our parents because we've got much more control over the situation. Even though we sometimes win a few of the battles here, in the end we lose the war because we really aren't strong enough or smart enough. This sort of thing goes on and on as we are growing up, and no matter how angry we get with our parents we can never really do much about it. Eventually we seem to have to fit in with what more or less pleases them. If we know what pleases them, we are very lucky, and we can develop a sort of way of behaving that is the same every time. Often though we are not sure from one day to the next exactly what is expected of us and so we get more and more frustrated, more and more angry and sometimes even depressed trying to work out exactly which way we are supposed to behave. Just sometimes we will be able to do more or less exactly as we want, and just as we think life isn't too bad after all our parents will suddenly explode and usually be very angry with us. It's as if we should have known all along how to behave.

It isn't too long before we work out that we've got to have some sort of method for dealing with the feelings inside us, and if possible avoiding our parents' anger at the same time. One of the ways, which we often use, but which is not very successful at all, is to get certain kinds of illnesses. Sometimes it's just a particular kind of symptom and usually it is headache[1] or tummy ache[2]. But at other times we begin to develop things that later on in our lives are called ulcers and asthma and colitis. These are all things that happen to you when instead of showing how you really feel, you sort of swallow it all up and push it down inside you. Nobody ever thinks that you are an angry person or a tense person. Often not even yourself. Anyway if you do realise that you have feelings as strong as that, you probably think that you are a bad person and deserve to have whatever illness it is that you've got as a kind of punishment.

[1] See *How to handle your parents when you get tummy aches*.
[2] See *How to manage your parents when you have headaches*.

Of course the better way is when we are able to really show in our actions the way we feel. When we get a chance to really use our strength I don't think anybody should blame us for trying. In the beginning we usually only do this with our toys, and especially with any toys that look like people, such as dolls and teddy bears and things. Later on we might be very nasty to any pets we might have like the dog or cat, especially if they are little. After that we usually try to be aggressive with our brothers or sisters and then eventually when we are really confident we try it out on our friends, often at school.

Being able to show how angry you are is easier if you have had a good example at home. If your parents are always being angry with each other in ways that you can see, and particularly if they hit each other, or if they hit you, then you learn about this and you think it is O.K. to do it yourselves. In fact the more your parents bash people about the more likely you are to do the same. Of course it's hard to hit back when you are at home and they are all so much bigger than you are, so unless you are stupid you find someone else to do it to. Often when we do these things our parents will get terribly shocked and will punish us for it. But of course this doesn't often work because we more or less expect to be punished, and the next time we will just be a bit more careful about whom we hit. We have grown to expect that kind of thing from people who are stronger than we are.

You will often hear parents calling us 'little savages' or 'primitive little monsters'. This of course is true in a way because, especially when we are little, we have all these feelings that we want to do just as we like. Feelings like this are very hard to control. If our parents know this they will try to encourage us to control ourselves but not without showing that they can manage to control themselves.

If the only reason that we do things for our parents is that they are bigger than we are, we will spend nearly all our lives waiting till we can meet them on equal terms. Some of them seem to know this and get terribly frightened about it ever happening. Then they bully us even more. The way to stop us bullying is for them to stop bullying themselves. They will have to stop some of us by force because some of us have learnt our lesson in bullying so well we just have to be a bully, and sometimes a very aggressive and dangerous one at that. No parent can really afford to have a child like that. It may just happen to bounce back at them. But if your parents are ready to change their ways, stop bullying and be very firm and logical and consistent with you, it might even work. Of course, we want them to tell us why they have changed their tactics and maybe even show us what else we can do with our angry feelings. The best way to show us is to do it themselves, control their angry feelings.

But if our parents keep insisting that the only way they can control us is to be bullies, then there is a very good chance that we little savages will just grow up to be big savages like some of our parents are.

How to manage your parents when you do poos in your pants

Well, there isn't much to do about your parents, because you will find that your parents will be very busy trying to do things about you. Once you have made a poo in your pants, it isn't your problem any more, it's theirs. Of all of the things that you can do to upset or embarrass your parents, particularly your mother, making poos in places where you are not supposed to is about the greatest. In fact parents feel so bad about this sort of thing that they very rarely complain about it to the doctor. If you just wet the bed, or suck your thumb, they might go and get some advice about it. But to admit to anyone that your little boy, who ought to have got beyond this, is still making poos in his pants seems to be an admission of failure very few parents can allow themselves.

There are a few different sorts of ways that this thing can develop. Sometimes some of us don't really ever seem to get used to the idea of doing poos in the right place at the right time. When our parents keep putting us on the pottie, we either get off and wander around, or when we find out that this is likely to get us a smack, we just sit there and wait until our parents are satisfied. Then we get up and make a poo somewhere else. This sort of thing just goes on and on and then by the time we are about seven or eight our parents give up and take us to the doctor. Of course when this happens our parents are pretty angry with us and they let the doctor know this in no uncertain terms. Sometimes the doctor will be terribly clever and find out that we have some little thing wrong with us like constipation or some funny thing wrong with our bowels and sometimes he can fix it up pretty quickly. But mostly he can't find anything wrong and that's usually when the trouble starts. The doctor is often a bit angry himself because very few adults like to know about dirty and messy things. Somehow or other they can pretend that they never did anything like that themselves, and if we dare to remind them that they once did, they get all upset about it.

Sometimes it's just a sort of smudge on our underpants that shows what has happened, and other times its the whole business. If we are very worried or anxious about it ourselves, we will often hide our underpants around the house, or do it up in little parcels. This of course is dreadful because the one thing you can't hide is the smell and sooner or later you are found out.

No-one really likes to have the smell of poos around all the time. Somehow this is what our parents and in fact most people find hard to understand. 'How can he possibly put up with it?' 'You'd think he'd notice the smell,' 'He must smell himself,' are all kinds of things parents say. Of course they're right, you don't like the smell either, but you like other things even less. You've got to choose between being angry right out in the open—telling people to drop dead, shut up, or that you hate them—and that smell. You choose the smell. After all, once you've said those things there is not much you can do about it. It's right out in the open. No-one else but you said it. But you can kind of pretend to yourself that you don't notice the smell, or even kind of pretend it was someone else.

It isn't only the smell of poos you have to put up with, but the feel of it in your pants, the difficulty you then have in walking and sitting and having to clean the poos off you. Nobody really likes those things, even babies don't. No one really likes to touch poos, to play with poos, smear it all over the place, sniff it or even eat it. Some of us do all those things. If you watch babies or children playing with poos, I'll bet you'll never see them doing it with a real delighted 'I'm having a good time' look upon their faces. They seem to either look pretty blank, kind of detached from it, or they look angry or disgusted. Perhaps most often they look triumphant. That's the way to look when you are doing something to someone else.

It is when we are babies that we learn that poos is something to do with feelings. We watch mother's face when she is changing pooey pants, we watch the faces of other people around us at the time. We watch, we feel what's going on. Anger, disgust, triumph, interest or detachment. They are some of the feelings most of us have about poos. We learn these quite early. Poos and these feelings get so mixed up together you maybe can't tell which came first.

To do poos in our pants we've really got to lose control of ourselves. Sometimes when we lose control we go all queer, or we get to be real excited and kind of take off, and sometimes we even lose control so much we don't know who we are or what we are doing. But poos in pants loss of control is different. It's a kind of controlled loss of control. It's a way of doing poos in the wrong place and for the wrong reasons and at the wrong times. Even if it's wrong it's still doing poos for a reason. The usual reason is that we poo in our pants instead of pooing on someone else. 'I'll poo on you,' 'I'll pull down my pants and poo you,' may be pretty much our favourite sayings when we are three or four. It would take a fair bit of control to be really direct and aim our poos, so as to hit someone we didn't like. It takes less control, but still some, being able to hold back our wanting to do poos till we happen to be out in the car or sitting up in bed or maybe in the bath.

So poos in our pants is really controlled, directed and aimed, but also it's fired. It's fired straight at those adults whom we want to get our own back on. Mostly these adults are our parents. Even if we don't always feel angry with them, when we do poos in our pants it's one time we certainly feel anger. In fact, to be able to poo on someone takes a whole heap of anger. Why does this anger pile up? It's usually because our parents are especially concerned with some things and forget about others. They want us to be neat and tidy, clean and well mannered, on time, punctual, exact and hard-working and above all to do poos nicely, quietly and without any fuss or bother. Poos must come every day, not only on time, but always at the same time. This they demand as a sign of our obedience, it is our obligation to them. They forget we are children. Children are untidy, slovenly and dirty. Children have no manners, no sense of time, like to play but hate work. Poos is a thing that we have to do. The sun rises every day, we learn the earth moves around the sun, the moon and stars appear at night time. Just as surely we have to do poos, but it does not have to be at the same time, nor every day nor even every week. Given time we'll do poos. If we leave it too long it hurts us. We learn not to leave it too long, we don't like to get hurt. If it's more convenient to do it after breakfast we learn to do it then. If we get to be real smart we notice every time we have a big meal we get the feeling of wanting to do poos. So we have to learn to leave the table to do it, that is, if we are allowed to do this. Then we learn to wait till just after eating. Anyway, that's what we'd like to do. If our parents let us kind of be children and control our bowels we get on all right. If they can't let us be children and even try to take over the control of our bowels from us, then we feel like pooing right on them.

It takes a bit more than this. We have to get so annoyed and angry to want to poo on someone and also have no alternative. Usually if people make us angry we try to find a way of hitting back at them, but we are small and weak and our parents happen to always be bigger and stronger (at least until we are adolescents). It's pretty hard to hit at them. If we do we know we will only get hurt even worse, especially if we have parents that lay down lots of rules. They always seem to be even bigger and stronger than anyone else. We aren't fools, we know when we are allowed to get angry and when we aren't. There are even rules for that sort of thing. But no-one, just no-one, can stop us from doing poos.

If we do poos in our pants one of the greatest punishments that parents and doctors cook up together is to give us an enema. This is a terrible thing that they do, where they stick a great big tube in our bottom and pour all sorts of sticky, gooey messes into it. Somehow or other this is supposed to stop us pouring gooey sticky messes out of it. It is such a terrible business that if we are just doing it on purpose, which is sometimes true, then we are likely to give in pretty quickly. The interesting thing about enemas is that some parents really seem to like to do it to their children, and sometimes they do it even when we don't need it. The whole thing is really pretty unpleasant, although if we get a lot of it, we can sometimes even grow to enjoy it, and that's even more of a bother.

However, by the time we get to the stage of having treatment, it's usually a pretty long process. By this time we are dead scared to show how we really feel, and it takes a long time before we sort of come out of our shells. Of course one of the troubles is that, if we do, the whole pattern sort of repeats itself, because our parents get angry with us as they have always done. Sometimes though, as we are getting closer to being teenagers, our parents will allow us to express the ways we feel more openly and to be a bit more naughty, and when we are able to do it this way, we sometimes find we don't need to do it that other way.

How to educate your parents when you have started being too clean

When we are going to school we gradually learn the rules of living with other people. Many of these rules have been told to us ever since we were pretty small. Before we go to school we have listened to these rules and usually said they are not good. Maybe we have kind of accepted them a bit, but usually we try to make our own rules or accept none at all. But going to school has lots of new rules connected with it. You go in the morning, start at a certain time, have your day divided up into neat little parcels. Some of these times are for play, some for work. Play gets to have rules tied up with it. Instead of just everyone for himself kind of games, we now learn to take special roles. Teams get picked, sides chosen and competition starts. It's the same with work. You work for a certain amount of time within a special framework laid down for you. Work gets to have rewards, only rewards according to a formula. So much work pays so much in return. Money becomes the way of getting a reward. We get paid pocket money when we are little, not because we earn it but because it's fun to be allowed to spend it. Gradually we might find that if we tidy up our rooms, wash father's car, mow the lawn, clean our shoes, wash the dishes, help set the table, run the messages, we get money. Pay takes over from pocket money.

Some of us get to be very conscientious. We do everything that is expected of us. Mother tells us to go to bed—we go. Father wakes us up—we jump out of bed. Big sister says get the milk in—and we hop into the cold rain into which she would not go because it would mess up her recent hair-do. Teacher says clean the blackboard—we obey. Never do we say no, never do we allow ourselves to answer back. We don't climb trees because we might tear our clothes. We don't play in the dirt in case our shoes and socks get smudged, maybe we don't even pick our noses any more or scratch our bottoms if they itch or dare to wipe our bottoms with only one sheet of toilet paper. We are so damned good it isn't healthy.

We are building up for a fall. We have got to because all those feelings we have talked about before, feelings we have had for years and years, don't just evaporate. They're still there, but they are locked in, they get to be closed off. We don't allow ourselves to let out angry words or actions. We stop any kind of sexual things from sneaking out into our behaviour. We get to be more and more tense, we're filled up with feeling, so full we could almost burst. Some of us do. It's all because of these rules. It's because at this time, the time of rules, those angry and sexual feelings we have cannot easily be expressed. They can't because we now have rules for these things. These rules are hard to duck, especially if we are not sure if we should be children or grown ups. We kind of like to follow the rules grown ups have, but we aren't really old enough, wise enough or game enough to do that. It would be nice to go back to being a child, being free and easy and not having any responsibility, and not caring over-much about the rules, but we can't. The rules won't let us. What do we do now? We can bust and throw out our rules, get back to being little heathens—no rules, just games, no work, just play, no pay, just pocket money (if not provided then it's got to be stolen), no school, just wagging it. But not all of us do this. Most of us go on hoping that as teenagers we'll get a better deal from those infernal rules. Some let out their feelings in other ways. Not doing what we want to do, just finding a substitute for it.

Sometimes this comes out in being too clean. We wash our hands over and over again. We go to the toilet and wash our hands. We wash several times after meals. If we should touch someone else we go and wash our hands. Should we inadvertently touch our bottoms, straight off to the bathroom we go. Each morning and each night, but four times on Saturdays and Sundays, we have showers, not just ordinary showers, but showers that last so long there is no hot water left for the rest of the family. We can't use anyone else's towel. If food falls on the floor we never dream of eating it. If our knife or fork slips off the table mat we demand new eating utensils. Why? We're terrified of germs. There are always germs around. We've known about them for a long time, but suddenly they take on a new meaning. They are the vehicle for our being unclean, the proof that we have not only unclean habits, but unclean (dangerous, uncontrolled, unacceptable) thoughts and feelings. The germs take over in our way of thinking as substitutes for our own actions and thoughts. They are the cause for our being unclean, not ourselves. We blame everything on to them. Instead of being able to control our thoughts we have to control our cleanliness and so stop the germs from getting us.

Sometimes our thoughts keep coming out, keep annoying us, keep on being repeated over and over again. These thoughts might not really be bad, it's we that see them as such. To stop them we try to put other thoughts in their place. Instead of thinking I'd like to hurt mother, over and over again we might make ourselves think red follows blue, blue follows yellow, yellow follows green, and so on. At times it's not only our thoughts we can't handle, but also our actions. Instead of letting ourselves get dirty, or letting ourselves get dressed in clothes we don't really want to wear, even allowing ourselves to go out to play, dance and sing, we do things by numbers. We touch every second lamp post or count every window pane or the number of blue cars on the road. Eventually we might have to do many things by numbers. Wash our hands twice, then four times, then eight times, then sixteen times, till maybe we just spend hours and hours just doing that. At other times we learn a routine. We put on the right sock first, then the left, then underclothes, shirt, or blouse, pants or skirt, belt or tie and then shoes. If we make a mistake we strip and start all over again. Maybe before we go out of the front door we have to touch each piece of glass in the hall or skip back and forth over the doorstep several times. You'd reckon this type of behaviour would get us into trouble, that people would notice what we are doing and see it as rather odd. The only odd thing is that very few people do notice it, sometimes even our parents don't until we tell them.

For many of us this kind of behaviour becomes our way of life. It's part of us, a part that never goes. It's our way of handling everything, every kind of idea, and every kind of feeling that is at all unpleasant, or that we are in any way unsure of. I suppose the most marked kind of this behaviour we find in some adolescents. They get to be so involved with making sure they do nothing outside the rules, rules they have made and remade over and over again, that they live the life of a hermit (and whatever girls are instead of being hermits).

Of course it's not wrong to have rules and in fact when we are children we usually like to feel someone whom we love and trust will guide us and help us to understand what things we can do and what things we can't. But there is a lot of difference between being guided and being restricted and this is what some of our parents never really seem to understand. Some of our parents seem to just let us go without any help or guidance at all, pretending that in this way they allow us to use what they call our 'free expression'. Often of course it's just that they can't be bothered with us. And the others all seem to go the other way and make up so many rigid and unalterable ways of doing things that we can't possibly feel anything else but angry at them. They seem to be saying all the time, 'I do not like him as he is, I am going to make him into the sort of person I will like.' Then when we begin to show the effects of this nobody gets worried about it but ourselves. People don't usually complain, and our parents aren't over-concerned. Their children are not anti-social, they are not breaking any laws, so they can sit back and relax and even feel proud of what good children they have.

Being a bit like this is a good thing of course, and if we are what adults call 'conscientious', we will usually do well at our work and whatever it is we want to do when we leave school. But when it starts to get out of hand, and we don't have time to complain because we are too busy counting and sticking to rules, then we are back in that position of being ready to burst. Then just as our parents are starting to feel safe, they will find they have been sitting on a time bomb.

How to handle your parents when you are shy

Being shy is a painful sort of business. Usually being shy is just part of growing up, but often it gets dragged out so long that it can become unbearable. One of the worst parts of it is that your parents, instead of wondering why it is that you are shy, and why it is you find such a lot of difficulty in mixing or playing with other children or talking with adults, seem to get very embarrassed about it. This is one of the things that you must never do to your parents, because if you make them seem foolish to other people, they are not likely to forgive you.

Somehow or other most parents seem to expect children to grow up to be very gay and bright, self-assured and confident children. When we don't quite measure up to this, our parents seem to feel disappointment. It's as if we have let them down. Of course sometimes we do, and we do it on purpose. Like when our parents bring us out in front of a whole lot of their friends and tell them proudly how well we can sing or recite. This is the kind of situation in which they are just asking for trouble and of course we often give it to them. When we don't do what they expect of us they say, 'Oh, he's just shy,' or 'Being in front of all of us has made him a little bit embarrassed.' What they actually mean is that it has made *them* a little embarrassed, but instead of accepting ridicule for themselves they kind of blame it on to us.

There are all sorts of reasons why we are shy. The interesting thing is that most of our parents felt the same way at some time or another. Sometimes we just haven't had an opportunity to mix with other people much, and seeing them altogether is a new sort of experience, and one that we have to learn to deal with slowly and in our own way. Sometimes our shyness is to do with being afraid of things that we don't know or understand. We often have all sorts of fears and fantasies about being looked at. Because no-one is really interested in listening to us we keep our ideas to ourselves. Sometimes we get to keep ourselves away from ever being looked at so much, we get kind of isolated from other people. There is no doubt that sometimes we do this just to upset our parents, or anyway to make sure that they are paying attention to us. So sometimes our shyness gets sort of exaggerated so that again we don't seem to be able to mix in any really worthwhile way with anyone. In a few of us this might be because other people really bore us. If we have really got a lot of brains, being at school might not be much fun, and certainly talking to most of the other children is not our idea of an interesting time. We often go off by ourselves to read or sometimes just to think and in a way you can't blame us.

The trouble starts when we start to prefer our own company to that of other people all the time. This is when we can get lost in our own thoughts and after a while we find it difficult to break away from them. The sorts of ideas and feelings that we can think up in our own minds are often more interesting and attractive than real life, and it is easier to escape into them than to come out of them. This is also true when the sorts of families that we live in are so frightening or so upsetting that they are almost impossible to face up to. We really get to run away into ourselves as a way of feeling safe. This gets to be called being shy, too.

When things are really very bad, some of us will even break off all contact we have with real things and real people. We get to be so sick that we sort of live all shut up inside ourselves, keeping out anything that is in any way unpleasant to us, so much that we might not even move and hardly breathe. We don't seem to hear people around us and sometimes not even to see them. If we talk at all, sometimes it is in a sort of private language and to our family we become strangers and sometimes we are even strangers to ourselves.

We aren't all so sick if we are being shy. To some of us it's just part of the way our whole family works. That is we live with adults, the important adults in our lives, who are also shy. They might be frightened or ashamed or feel inferior or even feel persecuted. They keep themselves away from people and in the process keep us away too. So we kind of grow up shy.

It's hard for our parents to be sure if we're being shy because we are sick or because we are just being ourselves. It's apparently even harder for teachers to know this. Quite often teachers are glad if we are shy—at least we are no trouble to them. Usually there are enough kids

who give their teachers so much trouble the teachers wish the trouble-
makers were shy too. Sometimes we wish our teachers would recognise
we are shy and try to get through to us. Being shy is painful. It is also
painful to stop being shy.

Making contact with people is hard for all children. Some of us get
over it by being so active everyone has to take cover or get killed in the
rush. But most of us who are really shy can't rush this business of making
contact. So it's better to proceed at a snail's pace—not really a snail's
pace, just at our own pace. We would wish that everyone could accept
us in this way; in our way, even if it is a kind of slow motion getting
used to people. We also need lots of encouragement—not force, just
gentle and repeated reassurance that everything will be all right. If we
do, we'll come out of our shells. It's hard enough to be shy but it's
much harder to put up with being ridiculed about being shy. When we
are shy we wish that everyone kind of saw us as legitimately staying
behind our wall of shyness—staying there till it's safe to come out.
Being told to 'stop being silly', 'stop being such a baby, come and let's
have a look at you', is being asked to do the very thing that's so hard to
do. Snails pull in their heads if they get apprehensive. So do we, only
we have to manufacture our own shells. Shells made of shyness.

We are no longer children

How to tell your parents about your breaking voice or budding breasts

It's hard to have a breaking voice or budding breasts. In fact, it's about as hard a thing to put up with as I can think of. It's so hard most of us nearly don't make it. We nearly go under, we nearly give up, despair of ever being normal, feel we may as well be dead, reckon the world is looking at us or listening to us and that we'd be better off on the next rocket to the moon. How we get through is a mystery. How we also put up with, and at the same time, changes in our size and shape, the strange places that hair grows in, a new kind of walk, periods, enlarging penis, not to mention all kinds of queer feelings and thoughts and ideas, is a miracle.

When these things happen, adults call it puberty. It's when we become a teenager, not a child, nor yet an adult. We're the people for whom a whole new industry has been built. We determine fashions in clothing, music, language and every form of creative activity. It's impossible for a mere adult to really understand us, because an adult can't be like us, feel like we do, nor even do the things we can. Some adults try and fail. We annoy our parents very much just by being what we are. It is hard to get to be an adolescent. To be fair there may well be one thing that is harder to be—the parent of an adolescent.

They often think we are mad. We don't like to think about it because it's too close to the truth. They reckon that most of what we do is wrong, that all our ideas are haywire, that we aren't capable of being responsible, that we don't know right from wrong. The thing they find hardest to understand is that we won't seem to listen to them any more, that we don't respect them for what they are, that we no longer appear to feel obliged to them for what they have done for us. This is kind of a mortal blow to most parents. They have nurtured us since babyhood, protected us from evil, led us into a respectable, lawful life. It's impossible to disagree with them, they have done all these things, but they might not have learnt to understand us.

They may have to put up with a tremendous amount of trouble, just for us to grow up, to change from childhood to adulthood, to pass through our adolescence. But we are the ones who are going to do the changing, we are the ones who have all these new experiences, all these changes in our body and the revolutionary kind of loving, angry, and sexual thoughts, feelings and impulses to tolerate. Not only do we have to tolerate them, we have to handle them. It's not possible to do these without getting close to the borderline of madness, not into the land of madness, nor at the border, just close to it. That's how difficult it is for us.

It is impossible for us to behave consistently. We are unpredictable. How can it be otherwise if we have to be both child and adult, yet neither at the same time. We have to be full of energy to cope with all our tasks and have enough over to learn an enormous amount. We have to let our feelings out and keep them in; to love and to hate; to fight ourselves and our enemies; to be independent and also dependent; to talk freely with others of the world, men, machines and to be silent, dull, restricted. All these we have to be at the same time; all of this and more, a lot more.

I wonder if our parents remember how it feels to change shape? People who take drugs think they do it. If you stand in front of odd-shaped mirrors you appear to do it. It's not just changing shape slowly as happens when children grow or even when adults get fatter or thinner. It's changing shape virtually overnight. Boys and girls both change from having a kind of straight up and down look. Boys to being broad shouldered and with narrow hips, bulging muscles and a protruding penis. Girls' breasts come out, waists go in and hips bulge sideways. We've kind of lived with ourselves being straight up and down for a long time. Now we look like someone else. Our picture of ourselves, built up inside us, has to be made over. For a time there are probably several pictures there—one past, one present, and one future. Which are we ? Confusion can well arise.

To make it worse our faces change. Boys get beards, thicker lips, angular jaws and frowning foreheads. Girls' features soften out, they develop fuller lips and rounder cheeks. We look in the mirror and we see a stranger. Boys' voices go up and down and they rasp and squeak, roar and whisper. Hair grows under our arms and on our abdomens. Hair hides our genitals from our view. Our arms and legs and chest may get a lot more hair as well. We find it harder to walk the way we used to. We kind of slouch along or walk holding ourselves all rigid. If we are very concerned by our manly chest or bulging breasts we might even have to cover up by drooping our shoulders forward. Again our image of ourselves is altered.

For boys their penis has been important for a long, long time. Now it starts to grow, it gets bigger and thicker and longer. It frequently stands erect. At night time with dreams, in the day time with sexually exciting sights and often without explanation, it stands erect and feels full and pulsating. It's almost alive. Boys wake to find themselves drenched in sweat and a new kind of odour. It isn't just hard to take, it's also exciting, it's the kind of thing that makes boys frightened, ashamed and sometimes lose control. They might get to talk about their having a feeling like an atomic bomb inside. This kind of feels that they will blow up, just like their penis tends to get blown up. It's almost kind of necessary to have a safety valve. This sometimes is the feeling of wanting to blow up something, or set something on fire. Sometimes this feeling gets to come out into the open and buildings do explode and burn. This might happen through the need that some of us have to get rid of these exploding burning feelings inside of us, and particularly inside a boy's penis. By getting them outside we try to get rid of them; only we don't.

Girls get much more attention paid to them at this stage of their lives. They seem to have more to show for it. Just as boys tend to mature earlier and earlier, so do girls. They start to have periods these days some year or so earlier than did our grandmothers. In fact, the onset of periods is getting to be in younger and younger girls all the time and I wonder where it will all end. Most girls have troubles when their periods start. It is not always their own problems that make for trouble. Often parents are very concerned when a girl's first period comes. It's a time for a lot of changes. Now she is ready to have children and she needs to be protected, or so they say. It's the sign of becoming a woman. There's one thing that most women can't stand and that is another woman who is younger and may be prettier and perhaps more active than they are. So for a girl to become a woman may create problems of jealousy and rivalry with her own mother and with other grown ups. But even more importantly, for a girl's period to start is a sign of her being no longer a child, able to start realistically to plan for her own reproductive future. Her ideas may well be to get cracking right away, to try it out herself. That's not so uncommon, it does occur. But more likely she will be a bit apprehenisve about this new role of hers.

It probably depends mainly on how her mother feels about her own periods, her own sexual life and having children, as to how she prepares her daughter for the onset of menstruation. Many mothers feel a bit diffident about openly talking to their daughters. Their daughters catch the same attitudes, feel somewhat diffident about having periods. Some mothers are pretty free and easy with their sexual roles and find it no real bother to tell their daughters. Others are so inhibited they tell their daughters nothing. To wake up one morning or to be at school one day and to suddenly have a period, not knowing what was going on, can be a very very frightening event. Maybe it feels a bit like dying, like being damaged, or even like having a baby. It can lead to a girl never ever wanting to have another period or maybe to being so angry with her mother to be unable ever to feel warmly towards her again.

There are a lot of difficulties that can arise at this time of our lives. Boys and girls can get through puberty changes with only a small amount of apparent difficulty. If we don't have any difficulties, or rather if we don't show ourselves to be disturbed at this time, you can almost bet that in fact we are very disturbed indeed. It is the keeping in or suppressing of feelings that are connected with entry to adolescence that may show just how sick we are. It's being unable to tolerate an open display of feeling, because to show any feeling may lead to lots of trouble in holding back other more dangerous feelings, that is a sure sign of our being disturbed. Lots of us do this for a while. Some get around to showing feelings eventually, some never. If never then it's too late.

If we could wish for something special for ourselves and we constantly had the intuition, understanding, knowledge and depth of feeling we can express so fleetingly but so intensely as adolescents, we would wish for our parents to do three things for us. Firstly to bring us up so well that adolescence is to be a time of fun with only limited periods of disquiet. Secondly that they try to remember their own adolescence and how difficult it was for them. Lastly, if they can't understand us, that they don't try to join us and compete with us. Nothing looks quite as incongruous and embarrassing to us as our father trying to outdo us in dancing with a sixteen year old girl, or our mother dressed up in teenage fashion playing football in the street. All of us would like to have some explanation, some of us will need some reassurance, but none of us likes to be teased.

How to manage your parents when you are at boarding school

The first thing to consider is why your parents sent you in the first place. There are all sorts of reasons for this although most of them are what adults call rationalisations. That's a very good word that adults use when they don't want to tell the truth but aren't prepared to admit it.

The first reason that we are often given is that we have to go to boarding school because mummy and daddy have to work, which is absolutely necessary if we want to get the things in life that are really important. Therefore there is no-one to look after us, and so there is nothing to do but send us away to school. Most of us of course find this difficult to understand. We have the idea that the most important thing is to be with our families. If they ever bothered to ask us whether we thought it was best for us to go to boarding school or for the family not to have a car, there is no doubt about which we would choose. Of course nobody ever asks. Sometimes parents tell us that we have to go to boarding school because there are no schools nearby that they feel are good enough for us. Sometimes this is really true, but I think it is still a bit of touch and go as to whether the better teaching we are supposed to get at these special schools makes up for what we miss out on by not being at home.

Another reason that parents have is something that they call tradition. They say it's a tradition that runs in the family that all the boys and all the girls should go to such and such a boarding school. I think this is another way of saying, 'I had to put up with it, so you're bloody well going to as well.' But whatever the reasons that are given to us, that is, if we are given any reasons at all, most of us feel that our parents want to get rid of us, and we feel rejected and hopeless and depressed. Sometimes though, we are only too glad to get away.

At other times parents send us away from them because they have been 'advised' to do so by doctors. At times the doctors have our best interests at heart and feel we would do much better away from our mothers and fathers who just don't seem to be hitting it off very well with us.

The popularity of boarding schools shows just how many reasons there must be for parents to want us out of the way. Sometimes it's because they can't stand the fact that we are growing up a bit and are becoming a real threat to them. There is no doubt that one thing a parent cannot stand is to be shown up by a son or daughter who is brighter, and more handsome or prettier, or who, worse still, seems to be some sort of sexual competitor for the husband or wife. Let me warn you if you are a boy and your father thinks you are competing too much, or if you are a girl and your mother thinks the same, you just might as well pack your bags straight away.

The feelings that parents have about their children are often not all on the surface. Even though they seem to love and want us, there are often little things about us which seem to pop up to the surface when they begin to see parts of themselves in us. Parents will never tell you whether they really wanted you to be born, although sometimes, when they are in a particularly sadistic mood, they will tell you that you were an accident. They often laugh when they say this which is really because they are very anxious about saying it. It's very difficult to cope with indeed. Sometimes you will have been responsible for getting your parents married in the first place. Adults are a bit confusing on this point. Some of them seem to get married because they want to have children. Others have children first so they can then get married. And others have children and don't want to get married, but do. These are the worst kind because they often don't stay married but if they do they make you pay for it for the rest of your life. Probably one of the strongest reasons for sending you away is because your mother and your father don't get on well any more, and they don't really want you around to see what goes on. Who do they think they are kidding ?

Once parents have made the final step of getting us into a boarding school, they can never accept that it was a mistake. It doesn't matter how much we tell them that we don't like it, it doesn't seem to make any difference. We can cry or threaten to run away or become angry, but our parents always seem to have the answer. They will explain and cajole and bribe and even threaten us in return, until eventually it is quite likely that they will manage to disillusion and depress us till they are really in danger of losing us for ever.

Of course once we are at boarding school it often turns out to be a reasonable sort of compromise, because many of the people who look after us there, really do have our interests at heart. They are well meaning, although some of them are kind of different, some of them are pretty rigid, and a few of them are homosexual which is something you have got to watch out for. If it isn't the masters or mistresses it's the other fellows or girls. Although in a way it's almost part of growing up at boarding school sometimes it can contribute to starting off a lot of problems which it takes years to solve.

When we are in boarding school we tend to form very close and deep friendships. It's a sort of self-preservation that we have, something that we have to do to feel safe and worthwhile. We often form gangs and we become very secretive about this. We make it very difficult to become a member of the gang and devise all sorts of sadistic initiations so that it becomes a pretty exclusive set up. This is all because we are frightened of what we feel in ourselves as we are growing up, frightened of being alone and often disillusioned with the adults around us. But, as we said, boarding school and the adults who are there can give us a reasonable sort of compromise family.

I have heard adults talking a great deal about the fact that 'all men are born equal'. This is, I think, another bit of adult rationalisation because anybody knows that all men are not born equal. This is more obvious in children. Each one of us has different needs and hopes and inadequacies and strengths and skills. Shoving us together in groups and gangs and classes and dormitories is a sort of game pretending that we are all the same. What often happens is that it crushes the talented and annihilates the weak. But it's very good if you are mediocre.

For some of us boarding school can do a lot of good. It would be a good place for more of us if our parents, as well as sending us there to learn rules, would also stick to a few rules themselves. We'd like them to remember us and keep in contact with us, not forget about us. When holidays come we'd usually like to spend them with our parents, not be sent off to another kind of boarding school, like a 'holiday camp' or to other relatives and so on. Some of us at boarding school get to be called 'weekly boarders'. If we have to be boarders we'd probably all rather like to be weekly boarders. After all we need a break from our teachers just the way our parents seem to need a break away from us.

How to handle your parents when they have adopted you

Being adopted is when two people who are not your parents are pretending to be. Perhaps that is not quite fair because a lot of them do better than even your real parents could have done. Of course some of them believe that no matter how they treat you, they are doing you some sort of favour, because if they hadn't taken you out of the orphanage probably no-one would have. Probably these ones are never really aware of the fact that they treat you in this sort of way, and all the time they really believe they are doing the best thing for you. When you look at it like this it's probably even more frightening.

All children expect to have parents, and all of us expect that the people we are living with are the ones to whom we really belong. In the beginning it never occurs to us that perhaps we are in some way different from most of our friends, but often it isn't long before we begin to suspect that something is wrong. The time that we first begin to be suspicious is usually about five years before our parents think that we know anything about it at all. Somehow or other they feel that we will never find out and so a lot of them never tell us. Mostly we play along with this kind of make-believe, because usually it is well intentioned and we don't want to upset them. They don't really seem to realise just how many people are aching to tell us that we have been adopted. Often it is people who are very close to our parents, like their parents or their brothers or sisters. Sometimes it is the neighbours, sometimes it is the neighbours' children. This happens probably because people just don't seem to like to see other people living happily. They become sort of envious, particularly if they are not very happy themselves.

Probably the biggest problem about being adopted is that the kind of parents who want to have you have mostly got something or other wrong with them. Often it's only a simple thing, like not being able to have babies of their own, and this is probably the commonest reason. Still, not having babies is a funny business. It might be of course because your father or your mother has got some physical sort of problem which is important. But lots of times there doesn't seem to be any real reason, they just can't produce any children. Now these people often have a lot of difficulties about sex and what it means to them. Sometimes they get all mixed up about it and it's almost as if when they are women they won't let themselves get pregnant. You can see this because often just after they have adopted us, and we have made them feel happy and relaxed and confident, maybe for the first time in their lives, they become pregnant and have a baby of their very own. This of course is often very upsetting to us and might make a real difference about the way our parents and we feel towards each other.

The other sorts of reasons for adopting a child are not so common, but also are not so nice. Some people adopt us because they feel it's sort of a charitable act and they more or less owe it to the community. These are usually horrible parents who are always telling you how much they have done for you, but of course they never do anything at all, especially never love you. There are even some parents who will adopt you because they need somebody to work the farm one day, or because they want somebody to play with for a while. These people usually treat you as a sort of piece of equipment about the place and they are very nice whilst you are in working order, but if anything goes wrong they are likely to get rid of you if they can. Of course if you are lucky someone might adopt you because they have got lots of money and they want to spend it on you. If you can't be loved this is some sort of consolation, I suppose.

These sorts of people are also often just waiting for us to put a foot wrong so that they can point it out to us and to all the people around and blame it on wherever we came from in the first place. 'It's her mother's bad blood coming out in her, after all you know what she really was,' or 'His father was a rough type, you know, he was in jail, so it isn't very surprising to find out that he started to steal, is it?' Sometimes because these people feel different kinds of badness inside themselves, they will sort of provoke us into doing bad things for them. If we have been adopted, they are not stopped by the thought that it is their own child doing it.

Most of us at different times of our lives get very worried about how we are related to our parents and what sort of people we really are. The funny thing is that a lot of us who are really not adopted become quite sure that we are. This is a sort of a fear that we have, which often comes because we feel that our parents don't really understand us or even want to understand, or that their ways of thinking and feeling and behaving are so much different from ours that they could not possibly be closely related, or because we don't seem to be able to communicate with them at all. It seems there must be some real barrier between us. This sort of situation often comes about when we are starting to develop as people ourselves, and when we are beginning to feel that we would not wish to be like the adults who are around us. So we imagine that our real parents are not our parents, and we begin to have all sorts of dreams about what our real parents are like. Sometimes it gets to such a stage that we even run away looking for them, but of course what we are chasing is a sort of an ideal person, and it does not take long before we realise that they don't exist.

However, if we are adopted, and we find this out as we start to develop into real people, when who we are and where we come from really matter, then we get quite worried and perturbed over our real parents and why it was that they rejected us so much that we were never able to be with them. Sometimes we dream about them as terribly good people, and sometimes as terribly bad. Often we begin to think of ourselves as bad people, to explain why it is that we were left alone by them, and because there is a lot of badness inside all of us, we can easily get depressed and unhappy at this time of our lives. If we get an opportunity to meet our real parents we usually take advantage of it, but it isn't often that we are pleased with what we see. Somehow it is just never the way we imagine it would be, and all we see is a man or woman whom we don't know. Perhaps this is really a very important thing, because although we are bitterly disappointed for a long time, we begin to realise that being a father or a mother means more than just having babies.

So it's pretty important to us when we are adopted that we get as good mothering and also fathering as is possible. Despite all that I've said about bad parents, many of us are adopted by good parents. Perhaps the people who organise this adopting business ought to be pretty choosey over whom they give the job of being parents to. It seems that often all adults need is a good reputation to be allowed to adopt children, when what they should really have is good feelings about children. The reputation of being a good parent isn't earned till after you become a parent.

Once parents adopt you they can't really keep it from you. Mostly this leaks out without their intending it to. They shouldn't really bother because you know by their attitude and their way of handling you and their way of answering your questions, especially about family relationships, that you don't really belong. Not really and truly belong. You're different. You're 'chosen'. They'll make up fairy stories about your being chosen. That's about the hardest thing to take about being adopted—that unrealistic story about something that is a cold, hard fact. So while you still believe in fairies and their magic, make a magic wish that your parents tell you as soon as you can understand the true facts of where you come from.

How to manage your parents when they are separated

Parents are hard enough to deal with when they live together and love each other. But when something goes wrong and they live separately, sometimes miles apart, the problem is far worse. There is such a lot written about love, and what it is like to be loved and fall in love, that it sometimes comes as a bit of a shock to us to find that mostly it is just talk. It is hard for us in the first place to understand how two people who really love each other can ever be angry or cross with each other, but after a while we get used to this. But to find out that being in love can be a sort of a temporary thing, and eventually can die away altogether, is very upsetting indeed.

After all the love we have for our parents and that our parents have for us is something that usually doesn't change a lot, anyway for many years. Especially if our parents have been reasonably kind to us and have let us grow up and become people for ourselves, the sort of feeling that we have for them is always a good one and a useful one. The better the feeling we have for them, and the better the feeling they have for each other, the more likely we are eventually to be able to love someone outside the family, in a healthy, wonderful, lasting way. Being separated usually starts with little things that parents call incompatibilities. Somehow or other when they get married our parents will just begin to find out about each other, and sometimes what they discover is not too nice. Often when they see that something is starting to happen to the way they feel about each other, they decide that the solution to the problem is to have children, and this, of course, is a hell of a reason to get born in the first place. Sometimes though this works, although it's only for a little while, and they usually find that they drift apart in all sorts of subtle ways. Our fathers go off and spend more and more time with their friends, and our mothers spend more and more time with us. Although they will never admit it to themselves, things gradually get worse and worse and the feeling of love seems to grow into a feeling of disinterest, and then into a feeling of boredom and then irritation and then hate. Our parents think we don't notice this, and they mostly 'stay together for the sake of the children'. Usually they do, for as long as they can bear it, or until we are what they call 'old enough to understand'.

All sorts of people of course advise them that they shouldn't separate because it is bad for us, and I suppose in a way it is. If we never have a reasonable model of married life to see, we may never be able to have any sort of stability in our married lives, if we have any. But of course the other side of the problem is that we can see what is going on, sometimes long before our parents can, and when the end comes we are often very relieved indeed. Sometimes of course our parents have used us against each other in all sorts of subtle ways. This kind of makes us feel like we should be split into two pieces. Over all mothers seem to get the better end of the deal here and it's usually them we side with, especially if we are boys. I suppose this is only natural since for many years it is our mothers that we turn to and look to for everything that we need, and we are only too glad to side with her against a person who doesn't mean that much to us anyway until we are older. What isn't fair, though, is when we really love them both and they put us in a position where we have to constantly choose, or spy, or take sides, or listen to one or the other telling us how bad the other one is.

Sometimes things get so bad that we see our parents hitting one another and occasionally we are even made to watch this sort of thing. I wonder if our parents realise how frightening it is to run between them and standing as we do between two giants to look up and say, 'Please don't hit my mummy,' or 'Please don't shout at my daddy like that.' I don't think they can possibly realise just how frightened and unhappy we feel. Sometimes of course one of them is much worse than the other, and they treat us as badly as anybody else, and sometimes even worse. If we have been born in the first place to save the marriage, they resent us more, and if they got married because we had been born or were going to be born, they resent us terribly. There is no doubt about it, that sometimes living in a house like this is much worse for us than seeing our home broken and destroyed and our family withered away.

When the separation does come, they can do all sorts of things to us. Sometimes they will send us to boarding school and sometimes they will send us away to some relative or other. But often we will go to live with one or other of our parents, most commonly our mothers but sometimes our fathers. When this happens it seems to be something that our parents decide for themselves, without talking to us, or at times it's a person they call a judge, who they think has some kind of super-natural power, but who sometimes seems to send us to the wrong one. At the times when he chooses correctly, however, he then goes and mucks it up by making us go and visit the other one at weekends, or on holidays or things like that. This never really gives us a chance to settle down and we are always nervous and anxious, and never know exactly where we stand or what to expect. I suppose it is too much to hope that our parents, and all of the other people that seem to get involved when parents separate, will ever ask us what we feel or what we think or what we want to do. Of course they are right to think that it would be frightening and upsetting for us to have to go into places they call courts and to have all sorts of strange people ask us questions, but if they could find some nice kind person for us to talk to, I am sure it would help. Even some of those people called judges are nice, despite what our parents say about them.

The biggest problem that we have in managing our parents when they are separated is to try to make each one think that we love them the best. This is definitely not easy because it is usually not true. From the time we begin to see that things are going wrong in the home, we begin to take sides and to have favourites. The position that our parents place us in seems finally too much for us to cope with and instead of seeing both sides to every story, we find it easier to see everything in black and white, the way adults usually do. Living with a mother or a father is not the same as living in a family, and no matter what happens to us from that point on, we know we have lost something. If only it were really possible for parents to be quite sure of each other before they had children, I suppose these problems might not happen. But if they do, it would be reassuring to know that they could behave like adults, face up to their own deficiencies and problems, and not drag us into it. If they have to separate we would like them to do it quietly without any fuss or recrimination and to make very sure we understand what is going on, and then to give us a real chance to settle down, before we are asked to understand or handle whatever new and confusing world we find ourselves in.

But whatever way you look at it, we don't get much of a start. Sometimes if we are very lucky and very mature, and meet good and nice and loving people as we grow up, we seem to manage quite well and we live happily ever after. But mostly it is as if we don't really expect any of our relationships to last very long and so they don't.

How to handle your parents when you are establishing your identity

Parents don't often realise the individual and emotional problems that we go through in adolescence. They are more than aware of some of the obvious problems that we face and the obvious changes that occur in us, changes such as hair under our arms and on our chests (if we are boys) and around our pubic area. They know that usually, provided they haven't fouled us up too much earlier on, we will start to show some interest in the opposite sex. Sometimes they laugh about this and sometimes they just can't tolerate the thought of it at all. But probably the thing that they have most difficulty with is beginning to acknowledge that we are no longer children and that we have a pretty good personality of our own.

Adolescence is a time of trouble for all of us. That's normal. Most of us don't have any very big problems or conflicts and we seem to pass on to a good, healthy and interesting period of our lives without setbacks or worries or problems, or anyway without any that last more than a short time. But for some of us it is quite difficult to begin to experience the ability to trust and love people outside ourselves. We have up to then virtually only loved ourselves and our family. We often find it difficult to trust anyone else with the kind of information and secret thoughts and hopes and feelings and desires which have built up within us for so long. Confusion comes easier at this time of our life and we need all the help we can get.

Unfortunately often we find that instead of helping us our parents seem to stand in our way. They don't seem to understand that just because we are growing up we are not necessarily growing away from them. If we are boys our mothers find it a great problem to see us now as men, to see us thinking of other women and to see us needing mother's love and affection and warmth apparently less and less. They still keep trying to bathe us and feed us up and fill us full of good things. When we finally get exasperated and reject them they get terribly hurt and sometimes very depressed. In the same way fathers begin to have a lot of trouble over seeing their daughters go out with young men who they know will have thoughts just the same as they themselves have. Parents find it hard to allow their adolescent children to become independent and to have private thoughts and ideas and feelings. They begin to think that we are keeping secrets from them and they resent it, and sometimes make us feel so bad that we find we can't work or concentrate, or we become angry and refuse to do anything that they suggest whether we feel it will be for our own good or not.

As we see ourselves grow in height and weight and education and understanding, we feel that the pressure of living is getting harder and harder. There is a need both in us and around us which suggests that we need to become 'someone', to become a person, an individual with an identity. The problem for us is which identity to choose and what sort of person to be.

We are expected to become people. People do things like working and making money, and we expect to do these things too. But how and in which of so many ways can we do these things? We are expected to, indeed we expect ourselves to, find a job. Somehow these days we have to start making our minds up about this job business pretty early on. Sometimes before we even know what having a job is all about—certainly before we know what any special job is about. We often try to find out by playing the field, going from job to job. It's usually said we are restless and that work doesn't suit us. Maybe we don't suit that kind of work, even if our parents and the teachers, bosses and most other kinds of adults expect that we should.

Another thing that people do is play. Play is not only for children. But parents reckon it is, even when they themselves 'play up', and they get to use all kinds of ways of hiding from themselves the truth that they play too. Our play is special because it's suited to our age. Play is standing on street corners, going to dances, strumming a guitar, listening to records. Play is pushing girls into swimming pools, teasing boys. Play is a way we have of getting to have an identity. Parents have an identity and we must borrow bits from it. They don't recognise it if we do this, often believing we kind of alter it around to suit our own purposes.

Parents have children. This doesn't seem to be play to them, they mostly say it's hard work. We don't want the work part of it, but the idea of having children comes pretty early to us. It's a way of having an identity. Not one we are necessarily ready for, but after all what better way is there of getting ready to have children, of being grown up, of being an adult, than do all the things that get us to be parents? Things like making love. It's a bit confusing this love-making thing. Parents sometimes regard it as play and sometimes they don't. To us it seems better to forget about the responsibility that goes with it and just use it as play. For it seems to us a way of getting to have an identity.

Often it's hard to do this thing of establishing an identity all on our own. We join up with other adolescents doing the same thing. We do the same things so much we all look the same, sound the same, behave the same, dress the same, talk the same, maybe even think the same. We belong. Parents don't. We get in a group and maybe the identity of the group becomes our identity. Parents can't get used to that, they can't be part of our group, they can't have our identity. They often say we are going bad if we go with a group. They often say groups are gangs, and that this means we are criminals or gangsters, but it's only sometimes that we get to be that.

If we have been lucky we have started long ago to model ourselves on one or other of our parents, hopefully the one of the same sex. But if our models haven't been too clear cut or if our models haven't been at home very much, we can often get into difficulty. Worse still, having solved the problem for ourselves and decided who we are and what we are going to be, our parents may decide that this does not fit in with their idea of who we are. Then there is real trouble. We might become withdrawn and indecisive and we don't mix well or sometimes not at all with the more healthy or successful of our friends. We fail in areas where previously we have done well and we fall below the expectations of others and of ourselves.

Often this is the first time that our parents perceive that there is something wrong, but even now many of them will continue to bury their heads in the sand and try to pretend we are all right. It sometimes takes a complete failure on our part, or worse still some kind of catastrophe, to alert them to the fact that we haven't made it as people; that we haven't found out who we are or what we really want. When this occurs sometimes parents finally have their wish and they are saddled with us for the rest of their lives, one way or another.

How to explain to your parents why you are a delinquent

Being a delinquent is a sort of special category that we sometimes get put in. It isn't really the same as being a criminal like an adult is, I suppose partly because we don't always do criminal things. But a delinquent is one of those names that adults call us when we are starting to grow up. They seem to get very anxious about us particularly after we pass what they call our puberty. This is the time when they start to realise that we more or less are men and women, or any way that we can make babies too. They get terribly worried about this because they can't any longer think of us as children. So they start calling us teenagers which is O.K., or adolescents which is not so hot, or delinquents. Now a delinquent seems to be the sort of person who does the sorts of things that an adolescent talks about and the teenager dreams of. I suppose when you think of it that way it's a bit hard to say which it is worse to be.

It's easy to see how worried the adults are about us because of the way they act, and how upset and angry they get if we do anything that they think is wrong. In a way they are right to be so worried because when we are passing through this stage of life, we begin to feel for the first time a tremendous sense of our own power. This is the sort of time when we believe in things called ideals, which are sort of good ideas that most adults pretend they never had. We have a sense that we have to achieve things and do good things in the world and we feel that people must listen to us and that we must be heard. Somehow or other this is the time when we feel it is important to do something good, or if we can't do that to do something significant. One of the troubles we ourselves have over this is that we are often pretty vague and confused about our ideas, and that sometimes even if adults take the trouble to ask us what we feel or think or believe it comes out as a pretty incomprehensible jumble. It isn't too surprising that often we get pretty disillusioned with the world and the adults in it and eventually with ourselves. This is what adults sometimes call 'growing up', or 'maturing'.

But even though we might see for ourselves what a temporary sort of period this is we get pretty fed up with the fact that adults never ever take us seriously. If they don't ignore us altogether they just seem to pretend we are not there, or that we are not saying anything at all. Anyway they make sure we never ever feel that we are taken seriously. It is an interesting thing to wonder why they should need to do this to us. It might be of course that the sort of idealistic view we have of life makes them feel a bit ashamed. But probably the most important reason is that when you get to be an adult you seem to lose the gift of seeing your own faults, and they realise that we see them as they really are. Another reason why they like to pretend we don't exist is I think that they see us as a sort of threat to whatever power or authority they have been able to accumulate. We are younger and stronger and as they grow older we grow up and they feel we threaten them.

Once we are just about free from our parents and almost able to feel indifferent to them and independent from them, we might get frightened and worried and become more dependent than ever. In a way, we are disillusioned with them because we see that they don't always play fair, they don't live up to the ideals that they taught us and they don't seem to think any of this is wrong. On the other hand we know how much we still need them and their support. I suppose it isn't any wonder that our parents often get confused with the quick changes we seem to show, the quick likes and dislikes we have, and the ways in which we seem to grow away from them one day and can't get close enough the next. If they handle us badly at this time and don't see how disillusioned we have become they may never again be able to fill the role of our ideal adults, and we have to select someone else for this. Sometimes it's a teacher or someone out in the community whom we think we can respect. At other times it's one of ourselves, perhaps the leader of a gang or a group of us or any person who belongs in our adolescent tribe and who manages despite anything that adults can do, to get to the top.

As soon as we turn that corner and become teenagers it's as if our parents are just waiting for us to be adolescent and then to be delinquent. They almost expect us to somehow or other break loose into some tremendous sexual spree, or to get terribly aggressive and to lose control. It isn't any wonder that we tend to behave much the way they expect. When you are full of the feeling of power and independence, and no-one will listen to you and no-one will help you do anything constructive with the feelings that you have, you are more or less obliged to do whatever it is they seem to want you to do. I have a sneaking suspicion that some of our parents even get a great deal of pleasure out of watching us do all sorts of things that they either have done, or they wish they had done. They might even be proud of us, but usually this is in a way that only makes us feel worse. In a sense some of them seem to get a sort of pleasure out of the punishment that they give us afterwards. It's almost as if they push us into being bad so that they can punish us without having any conscience about it. Well, I suppose it is pretty hard to punish yourself just because you have bad thoughts. It's a lot easier to punish your son or daughter or, better still, somebody else's son or daughter. The interesting thing is that it seems that all families only need one of us to become delinquent in order to get rid of these bad feelings. It's almost as if that one carries out the bad thoughts of everyone else. That it is almost necessary if the family is going to function properly. Perhaps society needs its criminals after all.

Adults seem to have been angry with delinquents for centuries and they always seem to have been saying how bad we are. I wonder if they are really angry at things we do or because we have dared to attempt what they can't do themselves. You know in many ways I think we are more puritanical than they are, we are certainly less hypocritical. There are all sorts of gangs, of course, and all sorts of reasons for belonging to one. Protection, fear, the need to have an identity we can claim as our own, cowardice. Mostly the things we do alone or in gangs will arise out of our confusion and out of the expectations of the adults around us that we will do unacceptable, bizarre, ridiculous, stupid, and sometimes frightening and aggressive things. But sometimes our delinquent behaviour is bad behaviour carried out by those of us who are a hard case of being apparently unfeeling, uncaring, violent and bigoted. Sometimes there seems to be no understanding it, and it leaves a heavy uncomfortable feeling in our hearts and our stomachs.

The most upsetting things seem to go together. How fast we become disillusioned and how short our memories are! Everybody seems to like adolescence to be a sort of period to be hurried through. The awful truth is that if you insist on trying to change from an adolescent to an adult you eventually become one.

How to manage your parents when you are promiscuous

The first thing to remember is don't tell them. Anyway don't tell them if you are a girl. If you are a boy it doesn't seem to matter quite so much. In fact you might even get quite an unexpected response particularly from your father. He will probably put on a rather stern expression and then, when your mother isn't looking, sneak up to you and whisper, 'You're a chip off the old block, son.' Those of you who are boys will know that it seems to be more or less expected of you to get some kind of sexual experience whilst you are still what they call adolescents and somehow the sooner the better. Sometimes all sorts of pressures are put on us either by our friends or our parents to make sure that this happens sooner or later. To some of us it is pretty easy, the opportunities are there and we don't worry too much about it. To others though it can be quite a problem, and when it is we either pretend that we don't really want to or that we are saving ourselves for marriage, or else, we get very depressed indeed. A very few of us of course really don't want to and maybe that's another problem altogether.

If you are a girl of course the whole situation is changed. In this sex business somehow girls seem to get the least help from every way you look at it. Not only do parents expect a girl never to have intercourse until she is married, but often they don't even expect her to know anything about sex at all. Of course this very rarely turns out to be the case, but it seems a pretty unnecessary thing to do to leave her in the dark about everything. Girls who start to have their first period without knowing what it is often get a terrible shock. Parents don't seem to realise what it might mean to wake up one morning to find unexpectedly that you are bleeding. Mothers especially often don't accept that there is any problem about this period stunt at all. Often of course this is only what they say, but what they really feel is tremendous shame or embarrassment about the whole thing, or even sometimes a dislike for it so intense that they will do anything to make their daughters suffer a little more. These mothers are very sick and it's not uncommon to find out that their mothers before them were just as bad.

Often if a girl is told anything about the whole subject it is usually the bad things. Girls are told how bad boys are, how they only want to get their pleasure and satisfaction from a girl, how they will leave them with babies and how much it is all going to hurt. Of course a lot of this is kind of true, but the way a girl feels about it often depends on just how she is told about it.

Parents are really a bit strange about the whole business of sex, as you probably have already gathered. The sort of standards they expect us to follow are often not those that they have followed themselves or even that they are following now. Anyone can see in the newspapers or on the television the sorts of things that adults really do or apparently like to do. It's part of our disillusionment to find this out. They won't admit it to us or even to themselves. The sort of thing that I think we are often expected to do is never to have intercourse unless we are married and even then not too often once we have children. It seems pretty obvious that the people who made up these rules don't know much about sexual feelings and how they develop. When we are little of course the sorts of nice feelings that we have seem to come from many different parts of our bodies, and we can feel pleasures just in enjoying the sensations that come from within ourselves. After a while these feelings all seem to collect together and centre around one place. This is the part that adults call the genitals which is a sort of nice word to use I suppose. To pretend that none of us have any instincts is just rubbish. We all have them and we have to do something about them when we are old enough but are not allowed to have intercourse. Then we often masturbate, or if things don't work out quite right we sometimes use different ways of getting sexual pleasure. But most of us don't really do the things that our parents suspect us of.

When we are young we still believe in things like being in love, especially if we are girls. Mostly we don't "do it" with anyone unless we really like them or unless someone is really pushing us into it. Often when we are girls it is our parents and particularly our mothers doing the pushing. When they start openly worrying about us and keeping us locked in and keep us away from boys, but at the same time allow us to start dressing up in high heels and lipsticks and fancy hair-dos, they shouldn't be surprised by the sort of things that follow. But of course they always are. 'I just can't understand, she has always had the best of everything and she never learnt that sort of behaviour at home.' If even half the girls really did some of the things most of their mothers are afraid they will do, there would be little business for prostitutes or striptease shows. Luckily there still is.

Often of course girls learn about how to use themselves to get what they want. Usually they see their mothers doing this to their fathers. Sometimes it's to get a favour, or some money or some new clothes, but sometimes it is worse than that when it is just a sort of weapon that mothers use to frustrate and provoke their husbands. It's not a hard thing for a girl to learn, but it's a hard thing for her to forget.

If you are promiscuous and if your parents or other people catch you at it I don't suppose there is much you can do. It's very interesting that if you are a boy and you have intercourse with a girl who is under sixteen this is against the law even if she is the same age as you. The funny thing about this is that there is no charge, with the law as it now stands, which can be brought against the girl. However, if it is just your parents who catch you, I suppose all you can say is that you won't do it again, which of course is something that nobody really believes but almost everybody is willing to accept. What you really mean is you'll do it again but won't let them know you're doing it; or maybe won't let on that it's your free choice whether you do it or not. Either way you'll probably satisfy everyone who thinks themselves concerned with your promiscuity—your parents, the law, your partner and perhaps even yourself.

How to handle your parents when you are down in the dumps

Being down in the dumps is about the commonest problem that we have. It is usually called being depressed, which is a word that covers a lot of different feelings and lots of illnesses, and affects lots of people. Although our parents often won't admit it, we are people too and we get to feel depressed just like they do. Nowadays if you have never felt depressed you are not really with it, but if you are always feeling depressed you are certaii ly not alone.

If we look hard enough underneath this feeling of depression we always find that something special happened to us. We've lost or we are lost, we are losers or we are losing or we may lose. It's all a question of loss. We are called the lost generation, but we could just as well be called the depressed generation. Loss is at the bottom of all depression. It's got to be an important kind of loss, it's got to be a loss of something or someone, or somehow or somewhere significant to us, but it's still a loss. We might say it can't happen to us, it's only other people, but it does affect us to such a degree that we can really get down in the dumps. So much so that we might not want to live. Life without loss is not life, life with loss is not the life we want. But we are children or anyway we are regarded as children and lots of adults wonder whether things like this really happen to us. They do, over and over again. We keep on telling our parents that we have got this thing called depression and they keep saying, 'Don't be silly, grow up,' but what they are really saying is, 'Stop behaving like an adult.' It seems that they don't like to be depressed and they don't like to believe that it could happen to them or to us, but it does.

We feel this depressive trouble in a lot of different ways. To some of us it's 'there is such a weight on me', 'I feel all weighed down', 'my mind keeps pushing down on me', 'there is no life in me, I'm just so heavy'. Grown ups can recognise those words and some of them get to know what they mean. What they don't know is that if you happen to be on the move all the time, are constantly active, unable to stay still, can't be quiet and feel restless, you may have to because you feel this depression. To feel weighed down, to feel so heavy there is no life in you, feels terrible. It might even feel as if you will die, so you have to keep on moving. It's running away from these feelings, it's making sure they don't catch up with you. To be still, to be quiet, is the same as being dead. You have to move to live.

Living means being loved and love is like food. Without love we can't live happily and well. Some of us get to feel unloved—'no-one loves me, you can't love me because you don't give me', 'you never loved me, you only love her (him, them, it)', and so on. You all probably recognise these feelings and so do many parents. We all say these things and we always mean them, though some of us mean them more than others, sometimes so much we just don't feel it is worth while living. Usually this is when what we say is really true—feeling unloved and being unloved are both true.

It's also true that sometimes we are unwanted. It might have been a hard time financially for our parents; it might be they have ten of us and eleven is just one too many; it might be too soon; too late; too soon after the last baby; or too long after. It might be because they just don't want children. If we are unwanted, we feel unwanted. That's worse than terrible. Maybe it's worse than being unloved. If you are young and need to want and to be wanted, to be held and helped, you just can't feel unwanted. If you are unwanted you are no-one. If you are someone it's only because you want to be someone; because parents want you. If you are no-one you may as well be dead. It isn't just being unwanted in fact, it might be unwanted in imagination. Only imagination doesn't usually stretch so far without a bit of support from reality. The reality of even a little bit of being unwanted.

Sometimes we will go to all sorts of lengths to prove to ourselves that our parents can want us just a little. Often the only things that are left for us to do are bad things and wicked things and harmful things and aggressive things, all of which of course make our parents want us even less. But being noticed because we are bad is better than not being noticed at all. There is sometimes a kind of a satisfaction in being punished although our parents are often mystified by the fact that when they do punish us, our behaviour does not improve. They get more and more angry with us and the angrier they get the more depressed we become. Eventually we say things like, 'I will run away and never come back,' which is of course what a lot of our parents are hoping for, or sometimes when we get really angry at them, we can put part of our feelings of badness on to them, but not all: 'I hate you, I hate you, I'll kill myself.'

I wonder if our parents really understand how we can feel? Being depressed, being unloved and unwanted can all feel terrible, but to be empty is worse than all of those. It's bad enough to be no-one, it's beyond our usual kind of thinking to be nothing, to have nothing, to feel nothing, to think nothing. NOTHING. NOTHING. NOTHING. Empty, nothing, nothing and empty. You go to the cupboard, it is empty. You go to mother, she is empty. You turn to the sun, it is empty of warmth. The fire is empty of heat, the world is full of people who mean nothing. The clouds pour down their rain and you feel nothing. Nothing; empty nothing. We are nothing when we get nothing.

To be given once but not again is better, but knowing that once there was something and now there is nothing makes us feel sad. Sad at the loss of what once was, sad at what once would have been, or what might be but is not likely. 'I'm sad,' 'I'll be sad if you go away.' 'When you growl at me I get sad.' 'Sad is a bad, bad thing.' If you are four or even only three, but certainly if you are five or six, you'll be able to say sad. If you're able to, sometimes you'll need to use it. If it's there very often sad might turn to bad. To be bad can mean it's our fault, our fault we have nothing, and get nothing, but more often our fault that we want what we once had and maybe gave away. If we are adopted we often feel bad. We might feel that we were adopted because our mother could not look after us, or because mother could not love us. Surely if she had wanted us she could have loved us. If she could not look after us then, she would now. It must be us, it must be our fault. She can't love us because we are bad. How can she love someone who is bad. We made her go away. How bad we are.

To be so bad is to be worth nothing. Worthless and useless. We feel we are less than a person if we compare ourselves with our brother or sister and find they have more, or do things so much better than we can. We might say, 'I'll never be as good as he is,' 'It's no use my trying, it's not worth it, I can't do it.' We are saying I just can't be of equal worth or use to someone else. Often the someone else is mother. This fills us with a feeling that isn't pleasant to have. It's a feeling we'd like to get rid of to replace with a feeling of being useful, a feeling that we are of worth. We need to have an idea of our own value. It might not be a realistic idea, it might be built up on false grounds, we might over-value ourselves. Our parents show us their need for us to be of value, through their own evaluation of us, and we imitate them.

Sometimes we can't feel very fond of our parents, sometimes we don't even want to be anything like them, sometimes they disgust us. Teenage daughters are particularly prone to tell their long-suffering fathers that they are disgusting, often because fathers smoke, drink or swear, or more usually because they are rude or sexual. May be it isn't father who is really disgusting, but perhaps his daughter who is more likely to be somewhat disgusted with herself, with her own sexual feelings. This kind of disgust can quickly pass. Other disgust with ourselves stays on. To feel ourselves to be dirty or depraved or despicable is what may happen. We often feel our own selves to be only worthy of disgust. This is closely linked with another feeling we have and that is of shame. We really all get ashamed of what we have done at times. Sometimes it's not only what we've done, but what we think. Being ashamed and being disgusted lowers our opinion of ourselves. We no longer can estimate ourselves as excellent, very good or good, not even as just fair. We reckon we are lucky to be below average and really ought to be classified as failures. Again it might be our depression that is showing.

Sometimes it's hopeless, or hopeless is the way it seems. There comes, for most of us, but usually only after we get to be seven or eight or nine, the feeling that there is no hope. Before that you say, 'I hope I can; I hope tomorrow comes quickly.' As we grow we get to say, 'There is no hope,' 'What's the use of hoping?' and even 'I feel hopeless.' You might ask, 'How can we live without hope and how can we get to have no hope?' We try to be us, to grow and do things, to be as strong as father, as beautiful as mother, to learn, to play, to work, to have fun. We might try, but no matter what we try we're told, 'That's not good, why don't you try harder?' 'Do it again,' 'Can't you do better than that?' We try, do it again, strive to be better, but when we return for approval we get told that's no good, why don't you try harder, do it again, can't you do better than that? And so we give up. We cannot ever hope to win approval, to meet those kinds of demands and we get to be hopeless.

That's pretty grim, but it's even worse to be helpless. Little babies are helpless. They need to be looked after, to be fed, to be kept warm, to be given love. Babies know that whatever they need they'll get. They cry and demand and they get what they need. If they don't, they are truly helpless. If you aren't a baby and you feel this, you are feeling helpless. You ask and demand and cry for help and if it does not come, your feeling is 'I'm helpless'.

Helpless, hopeless, empty, useless, sad, depressed—where do they all come from really? From loss. Loss of something that's important, somebody that means a whole lot to us. We children can't ever lose anybody that's more important or means more to us than does mother. That goes not only for children, but for grown up children too. At times we lose mother because she dies, or she is very sick, or she is in hospital, or she has left us, or maybe she is so busy she cannot see us. Much more frequently it isn't that she has done any of these things, she is there all the time, mother is living with us. But somehow she is not quite full of life. We talk with her and she talks back, we smile at her and we might get a smile in return, we ask and we are given. But somehow it is not what we want, it isn't enough. We feel mother is not quite with us. She is depressed, part of her is there, but part of her is missing and empty and lost. So we demand more and more, but she just can't give what we ask and we wonder why. Maybe she does not love us, maybe we are bad, maybe we've made her angry, maybe anything. Not knowing is terrible. If only she would tell us what is wrong. We ask, 'What's wrong with you? Tell me what's wrong, are you angry, are you sick, are you sad?' We don't ask what we often wonder: 'Mother, are you dying?' Mother doesn't die, mother gets better. Mother smiles and laughs, so we smile and laugh. Mother is happy and we are happy. But underneath we remember that time mother was depressed. It stays with us and like a bad dream it kind of haunts us. Will it happen again, will mother be like she was? Maybe she'll die. We try to make up for that feeling, but how can we? Often we become insatiable. We demand more and more and are never satisfied. Nothing can satisfy that empty feeling, the feeling that there was not enough of mother. Mother was depressed. We stay depressed even if we don't show it.

Being down in the dumps is common to many mothers and it's common to us too. But cheer up, we're children, we're growing, we're changing, we're alive.

Index